Business in a Backpack

Visit our How To website at **www.howto.co.uk**

At **www.howto.co.uk** you can engage in conversation with our authors – all of whom have 'been there and done that' in their specialist fields. You can get access to special offers and additional content but most importantly you will be able to engage with, and become a part of, a wide and growing community of people just like yourself.

At **www.howto.co.uk** you'll be able to talk and share tips with people who have similar interests and are facing similar challenges in their lives. People who, just like you, have the desire to change their lives for the better - be it through moving to a new country, starting a new business, growing their own vegetables, or writing a novel.

At **www.howto.co.uk** you'll find the support and encouragement you need to help make your aspirations a reality.

You can go direct to **www.business-in-a-backpack.co.uk** which is part of the main How To site.

How To Books strives to present authentic, inspiring, practical information in their books. Now, when you buy a title from How To Books, you get even more than just words on a page.

Business in a Backpack

A step-by-step guide to building a business while traveling the world

Adam Costa and Darcie Connell

How to books

This book is dedicated to our parents
Dona, Dan, Mary and Ken
for their unending support.

We love you all.

Published by How To Books Ltd
Spring Hill House, Spring Hill Road,
Begbroke, Oxford OX5 1RX United Kingdom
Tel: (01865) 375794. Fax: (01865) 379162
info@howtobooks.co.uk
www.howtobooks.co.uk

How To Books greatly reduce the carbon footprint of their books by sourcing their typesetting and printing in the UK

British Library Cataloguing in Publication Data
A catalogue record for this book is available from the British Library

ISBN 978 1 84528 404 6

Produced for How To Books by Deer Park Productions, Tavistock, Devon
Typeset and layout by Baseline Arts Ltd, Oxford
Printed and bound by Ashford Colour Press Ltd, Gosport, Hants

Contents

Arrival: the business in a backpack lifestyle

Ha Long Bay, Vietnam. My wife Darcie and I awoke aboard a Vietnamese boat, surrounded by early morning mist. After breakfast onboard, we docked on Cat Ba Island for the day, walked along the beach and soaked in this amazing UNESCO World Heritage Site.

The past six weeks have been incredible: we ate frogs, drank on the street with locals in Vietnam, rode a motorcycle through rice fields, explored the ancient ruins of Angkor Wat, and scuba dove the crystal clear waters off several tropical islands.

The next six months will prove to be just as interesting: river trips through Laos, Malaysian cooking classes, Indonesian tribes, trekking in India and Nepal … and that's just the stuff we're certain to do.

As incredible as this trip has been, the most incredible part is that *we haven't spent a penny* of our savings. In fact, we've actually *saved* money.

This will continue for the rest of our travels. For as long as we want. Into perpetuity.

This is the result of working a helluva lot smarter – and a bit harder – than I had in the past. My wife and I currently maintain half a dozen websites, and are in the process of creating two more. These websites – which I refer to as 'streams' throughout this book – are the reason we are able to live the way we do.

We meet so many travelers on our adventures, most of whom are constantly short on at least one of the two most valuable commodities: time and money. Short on time, because they have responsibilities back home such as work, family, or school; short on money, thanks to mortgages, loans, or the shrinking of their travel budget.

Our situation is the complete opposite. Our streams bring in more passive income each month than we spend, which results in an interesting situation: we have copious amounts of free time and a never ending stream of income to travel with. We could be on the road for a month or a decade; it's entirely up to us, not predicated on a lack of time or money.

This is the business in a backpack mentality; that streams are the path to wealth, not just financially, but in the broadest sense of the word. Streams can provide peace of mind, and the ability to see the world from a new vantage point.

This book was written with the explicit intention of changing your life. I hope that you learn to put these strategies to work for yourself and start living the life you've always wanted. Humans are meant to explore the world around them; we are creative and curious creatures who grow only when exposed to new ideas, cultures, and ways of living.

This book isn't a travel guide. Nor is it a 'get rich in your underwear' book. This is a guidebook for how to set up income streams and manage them while traveling the world.

When I started building my online business, I worked as a travel agent and have extensive knowledge of the travel industry. In addition, Darcie and I have taught several classes on Internet Marketing. I have advised large corporations and universities as an AdWords consultant, and Darcie has designed websites for a number of years now. Lastly, we have spent more than a year traveling the globe while launching new businesses, from Ireland and Cambodia to Malaysia and Nepal.

We'll first look at how to set up your business so that it runs on near auto pilot. Then we will examine how you should plan your travels around the world. Don't expect recommendations on what's the best restaurant … frankly, I don't care where you go or what you do. What's important is that you go.

I'll show you, citing personal examples, how I manage to travel the world with my wife and still have money left over.

It all begins with a simple step. Are you ready to build your future?

HOW THIS BOOK IS STRUCTURED

This book is divided into four main sections.

1. **Inspiration** includes a listing of some of the most intriguing destinations around the world, along with colour photographs to get your imagination running.
2. **Education** contains comprehensive information on how to build an online business, from creating a product to accepting payments.
3. **Perspiration** provides step-by-step accounts of three very different online business models to finance your dreams. Pick one and get to work!
4. **Embarkation** covers the nuts and bolts of long-term travel abroad such as how to plan your routes, flight options, visa requirements and loads of other low to the ground information you'll need for your adventure. Finally, we'll tie in how you can manage your streams while traveling abroad.

This book begins with broad generalizations and concepts, gradually moving toward highly detailed processes. It is my hope to illustrate the *why* of this experience before delving too deeply into the *how*. For more information on the business in a backpack lifestyle, including videos on the topics covered in this book, visit the companion website at www.stream-life.com.

ONE

Inspiration – free yourself

In a past life, I worked as a financial planner, where I was taught the importance of saving and investing for the future. In all honesty, this is a half truth. In order to live life to the fullest and invest for the long term, you have to be able to *produce more income* than you currently live on. You must learn to value income over growth in order to realize your financial goals.

Value income over growth? No, I'm not talking about buying bonds. Rather, I'm talking about building a business online that provides substantial income with limited ongoing work. Once you've achieved this, you will be able to invest a proportion of your profits for your long-term financial goals.

A caveat: many people mistakenly believe that they can create a million-dollar business in a matter of mere hours. It's best to imagine your online business as a rocket: to get off the ground takes an immense amount of energy, but after that it is smooth sailing.

I grant you no illusions. You must be prepared for a long, arduous process of generating ideas, testing markets, creating products, building websites, developing relationships, and closing sales – all of which we will cover in this book. The good news is that once you've been through this process once or twice you'll have climbed the learning curve and built a foundation that can be easily repeated, thereby allowing you to create multiple streams so that your profits increase more rapidly.

THE END GOAL

We all have dreams of travel, and the purpose of this book is to show you how to achieve them. Whether it be drinking steins of beer at the Oktoberfest or hiking to Everest Base Camp, your goal should convince you there is a better life out there – one that can be achieved with the right mindset. Which activities have you always dreamed of doing? What places have captured your imagination? If you were lying on your deathbed, which experiences would you most regret *not* doing?

Marshall Islands
42

Wherever the road might take you, the method for getting there is the same. Choose a dream, write it down, and give yourself one year to achieve it. As you'll soon see, there is a way to live a life that others only visit in dreams.

MAKING 'THE DECISION'

December 8. This was the day I cracked. Working as a travel agent during the day, and a waiter at night was beginning to take its toll. Mornings began at 7 a.m. and, if luck was on my side, I'd get home before midnight. There was no time to spend with my fiancée, let alone friends and family.

I was trying to get the Saturday off in order to attend Darcie's annual company Christmas party. I couldn't miss it, and requested the day off from waiting tables. My boss said he would call me at 3 p.m. with the verdict. I'd already decided I was going no matter what the verdict was, even if it meant losing my job. Still, I didn't want it to come to that.

As Darcie was getting ready, I lay in bed waiting for the verdict. For the life of me I couldn't figure how I'd worked myself into such a corner. I needed to do something radically different with my life. There had to be a better way …

BAM! Like a blinding flash, I had an epiphany. I would create songwriting tutorials and sell them online. I could see the full product all at once: several audio CDs of instruction, instrumentals, software that included a thesaurus and rhyming dictionary, several workbooks … even special 'bonus' materials to offer people.

Suddenly, these two jobs were no longer a means of survival. They were hurdles to my hopes and dreams. They weren't paths to a better life; they were obstacles that drained my energy and affected my relationships with the people I cared most about.

They had to go. Immediately.

When the phone rang at 3 p.m. I couldn't have cared less. Turns out, I didn't have to work that day. They received my two-weeks' notice the next day. One year later, the travel agency got the same and I was heading to Asia for a year-long adventure with my new wife and life, funded by the streams we had created.

AUTOMATION IS KEY

Before we get into the step-by-step process of how to generate income automatically online, we first need to touch upon the concepts involved that must drive your stream. Notice how I use the term stream, rather than business, hobby, or investments.

As the old marketing adage goes 'businesses don't make people rich, systems make people rich.' In this book we define a business as an umbrella which includes numerous streams that provide passive income. Along every step of the way, you need to ask yourself how you can automate each stream in order to simplify your business.
The streams that my wife Darcie and I have created are fully automated. By organizing our processes, we achieved two important goals:

1. It allowed consumers immediate access to our products without our help.
2. It freed up time for us to travel and create new streams

Each new income stream will first pay for coffee, then meals, then travel around the world.

Freeing up your time is crucial to achieving your dreams. I would rather make $2,000 / £1,320 per month passively than work full time for $10,000 / £6,600; the former supplies me with enough money to see the world while the latter gives me a view of a cubicle. There are plenty of six- and seven-figure earners who can barely afford a two-week vacation each year. Is that wealth?

When you create a stream that produces income automatically, it really doesn't matter how much it makes. For example, I've built a website that generates three dollars a day like clockwork. Does this allow me to go skydiving in New Zealand? Of course not. But I don't have to get up and work for it every day. It's like having someone write you a check for $100 / £66 every month. Another website brings in about $25 / £17 a day; a few others bring in between $5 / £3 and $10 / £6 a day, all on autopilot.

On average, each new stream takes about six weeks to research, develop and implement. If you were to create a new stream at this pace, each bringing in $250 / £170 a month, you would have enough money to travel throughout most of the world indefinitely in less than one year. More on that later.

BEFORE YOU BUY ANOTHER INDEX FUND

As mentioned previously, I used to work in the securities industry, and part of my job was to analyze investments and determine whether the risk was worth the potential reward. People would be thrilled to receive 8% annual growth with limited risk. Now I know better.

The best investment you can make is in yourself. Rather than invest in assets such as stocks, bonds or real estate, focus on creating your own assets. If your streams cost $1,000 / £660 per month in advertising and manage to pull in $1,360 / £898 per month in revenue you are earning a whopping 36% monthly return. So much for the stock exchange.

If possible, pay for your business out of pocket, and allow all your revenue – not just the profits – to accrue in a separate bank account. You'll be amazed how quickly the money piles up!

This is how you can achieve returns far beyond anything you've ever imagined. Thanks to investing in yourself, you are able to accomplish returns that investment advisors could only dream of. Remember this key point as you develop your streams in the future, and keep investing in yourself!

OPEN MIND POLICY

I never imagined my wife and I would be traveling throughout Asia without touching our savings, nor that I would be writing a book showing others how to do the same. The key to our success, I believe, was having an open mind policy.

Many companies have what is known as an open-door policy. This states that those higher up in the company will always have a door open for their employees to come in and share their thoughts about the company and its intended direction. When developing your streams, you should learn to cultivate an open mind policy.

An open-mind policy enables you to keep the doors in your mind open to new experiences. It allows you to build on old projects and create synergies with new ones. Your previous streams can be significant contributors to your future streams; this book is a product of such a synergy – after writing extensively about travel and Internet marketing, it made sense to create a book synthesizing these two areas of my expertise.

An open-mind policy holds true for both building streams and traveling abroad. You may have planned a walk along the river, but remain open to the possibility of whitewater rafting should the opportunity arise. Learn to embrace spontaneity, or as Heath Ledger says in The Dark Knight, 'become an agent of chaos.'

Some business opportunities will make money and some won't. Some areas traveled will become lifelong passions, while others leave you running for the hills. The point is to learn and grow from the experience. Keep every door open and opportunity won't knock – it'll come right in.

Below are actual money-making events that happened for us by having an open-door policy. We:

1. Created an online business selling a downloadable product.
2. Created another online business following the same model as previously implemented.
3. Taught a class at a college on Internet marketing based on our experiences with the above.
4. Created another website based on the class we taught where we marketed ourselves as consultants
5. Created a content-driven website with advertisements where a user would visit our website and access free information, which currently brings in a few hundred dollars a month from advertising.
6. Consulted with numerous clients on website development and Google AdWords

And the list goes on…

As you can see, most of these steps were predicated on those completed before. By keeping an open mind policy, we were able to position our products and services in different ways to bring in more money without starting from scratch.

THE LEARNING CURVE vs THE EARNING CURVE

Starting a business is tough. There are so many aspects to familiarize yourself with that the task can appear daunting, if not insurmountable. At first, you'll feel severely underpaid, but as time goes by, and the quantity and quality of your streams increase, you'll eventually find yourself significantly overpaid! It's like any other industry: sacrifices are made educating yourself before reaping the rewards.

When I started, I didn't know anything, and my earnings reflected that. Over time I was able to learn from my mistakes, and improve my streams. Suddenly, I knew a lot, and earned a little. I could expound on dozens of topics related to Internet marketing and travel, but I wasn't able to use my knowledge of the former to make the latter happen.

This, unfortunately, is where a lot of people get stuck. Why? Because most people enjoy learning new things rather than doing the work needed to put them into play. You must put all your new-found knowledge to work in order to reach the underworked/overpaid echelon.

I wrote this book on Ko Lanta, an island in southern Thailand. Sure, I could have laid on the beach every day until I started to resemble George Hamilton, dreaming of the millions I would make with a lucrative book deal, but that wouldn't have moved me any closer toward my goals. That's why I made damn sure to crank out at least 1,500 words every day before cracking open a bottle of Beer Chang and watching the sunset.

It's like our physical appearance. It's great to look sexy, but sit-ups suck.

Without dedication, you are accepting failure. If you currently work full time, be prepared to come home, have dinner, and get to work on your future. I worked two full-time jobs – close to 90 hours per week including the commute – and was able to create and market my songwriting tutorials within six weeks. My life was the complete opposite of what I had dreamed it would be, and this fueled my dedication to create a better life for my wife and me.

Doubt inevitably creeps in. But don't give up! The key is to keep building streams. By continually creating new streams you are forcing yourself to think strategically, rather than get mired in minutiae. By following the advice outlined in this book, it is very simple to scale your streams so that you can earn $10,000 / £6,600 as easily as you can $10 / £6.

When we started out, things looked bleak. We were unprofitable for several months at first, and self-doubt was beginning to take its toll. I had read nearly every marketing book available, joined online forums and even hired a consulting team – for $1,500 / £990 – to examine my business model and make suggestions (which turned out to be even more unprofitable). Not only was I losing focus, it was beginning to affect my sleep patterns: my wife confirms that I would utter phrases like 'split testing' in my sleep.

However, all that education and perspiration eventually paid off. After the first month in which we made $1,000 / £660 profit, I finally felt compensated for all the hard work we had put into building our streams.

And hard work it was. You will have to work your backside off to make this business work. It's also an emotional roller coaster: one day you feel like a multi-millionaire, the next a complete failure (funny how a couple of sales can alter your perceptions so quickly). There have been days where we've made over $500 / £330 without working, and there have been days where we've lost $100 / £66. In the end, you should live on a daily budget based upon your average monthly income.

Don't beat yourself up. Set small, achievable goals early on and work toward them. Even if you're only making a few dollars a day on average, it's still headed in the right direction.

And it only gets better. Once you've created and automated a stream, you now have passive, residual income that rolls in while you work on other projects. Let's say you were able to create a business that automatically generated $100 / £66 to $130 / £90 per month. As you can see in Fig. 1, your work (input) remains level each month, while your revenue (output) increases. Unlike an 9–5 job, with your stream you could stop working and continue to get paid. Want to stop after a year? No problem ... grab a plane ticket to somewhere exotic and live it up with a few grand of passive income rolling in every month. Rather be filthy stinking rich? Create streams until you're a six- or seven-figure earner, build your dream home and spend your days wine-tasting in Burgundy. It's really not that hard once you get – and keep – going on the right track.

FIGURE 1 **WORK INPUT VS. MONEY OUTPUT**

TWO

Education – how to make money anywhere, anytime

You don't need to love what you do in order to make money, but it sure helps.

MONEY MAKING STRATEGIES

It's not just the topic, but also how that topic is presented. For example, I love kicking a foot bag (also known as hacky-sacking) around with my friends, but I'd be bored out of my mind if I had to write an e-book on it. However, what about a free website that offers video tutorials on how to properly execute foot bag tricks? Sounds like a great way to spend a weekend – at least for me.

Your heart and your personality are crucial to your ongoing success with building your business. Therefore, which stream you choose is in no way related to how much money you can earn. It is a personal choice that should reflect your passion and skill set. Let's look at three different streams for making money online, and the personality traits associated with them.

Method 1: Product development stream

A product development stream is developing a product (a good or service) and selling it online. In general, this entails researching a market, developing a product, creating a website, driving traffic to your website, and selling your product.

Product development is a great avenue for synthesizers and fire starters. It requires a strong, short-term focus, as well as the ability to create a quality product and get it to market as quickly as possible. If you see yourself growing bored with projects after four to six months, enjoy being the boss and are willing to risk a small – but not insignificant – amount of capital, this may be the method for you.

Product development can be very intense for the first few months; you have to create not only the product, but also the marketing materials associated with it before you earn a sale. While this may seem a daunting task, I'll show you ways to test a product and launch it within four to six weeks.

I created a product well over a year ago which continues to earn between $700 / £460 and $1,000 / £660 per month. Had the process taken longer than six or seven weeks, I never would have completed the project, due to a serious case of entrepreneurial attention deficit disorder – or ADD. Product development is a lot like working firefighters' hours: you work your backside off non-stop and then enjoy your time off.

You need a strong work ethic but not necessarily a dedication to the long term. I get really excited over a new project, but its appeal has almost gone by the time I launch it. To succeed in product creation, you'll need the strength and skill sets of a business owner.

Method 2: Content creation stream

A ***content creation*** stream involves creating large, content-rich websites and earning revenue from advertisers. This stream includes researching a topic, and adding new, related material to grow a list of subscribers.

I've seen several people, including the creator of the international train site Seat61.com create and maintain large websites based on personal interests, only to see those websites explode into a profit-generating powerhouse.

While creating a product relies heavily on a short-term all-consuming focus, creating a large content-driven website requires the dedication to create that content over several years. In other words, whereas product creation results in a flash flood, a content-driven website provides a steady stream.

Creating a content-driven website requires some serious elbow grease. You must be prepared to build your website into an authority that attracts large amounts of traffic – and with it, advertisers willing to pay you for the opportunity to market to that audience.

In a way, product creation and content-driven websites are the yin and yang of e-commerce. On the one hand, people create products and look for content-driven websites on which to market them; on the other hand, people with content-driven websites are on the lookout for ways to capitalize on their influence. Unlike product development, most content-driven streams are not promoted with paid advertising, which greatly reduces the financial risk (while increasing the ongoing workload).

People who create-content driven websites must have the same strengths and disciplines found in those who freelance for a living.

Method 3: Affiliate network stream

An ***affiliate network*** stream makes money building websites that offer prospects numerous different products sold by affiliate partners. A popular example is Amazon, which makes a commission on every product sold.

Building an affiliate network require skills from both ends of the spectrum. Those who excel at creating affiliate networks have a strong long-term work ethic, the ability to collaborate and maintain a wide variety of relationships, and a passion for what they do.

Unlike product development, an affiliate network requires no customer service. Rather than answering questions from prospects or handling returns, you will be responsible for building and maintaining relationships with other business owners.

The single most important trait of an affiliate networker is communication. If you aren't a people person, try another method. An affiliate network requires the same skills found in managers of large companies, such as leadership, communication, and focus.

Personality summary

Table 1 provides a brief summary of each stream and its responsibilities.

TABLE 1 **PERSONALITY SUMMARY**

	Product development stream	Content-driven stream	Affiliate network stream
Risk of capital (if using paid advertising)	✓		✓
Immediate startup	✓	✓	
Customer support	✓		
Ongoing content creation		✓	
Long-term focus		✓	✓
Manage business relationships			✓
Business dedication	✓	✓	✓

These three strategies can be applied to almost any idea – it's your level of dedication and passion for the project that determines which is the most applicable. I've created products for markets that don't terribly interest me, built content-driven websites on those that do, and maintained affiliate networks for markets that already have a lot of products. The key is to discover which stream works best for you.

Stream checklist

In order to succeed in your chosen stream, you'll need an arsenal of marketing knowledge and tactics. Table 2 shows a chart highlighting each stream's requirements, all of which are discussed in this book.

As you can see, product development requires the most comprehensive approach, and carries with it the greatest amount of control. Content-driven websites require the most elbow grease, but carry very little financial risk. An affiliate network stream is a compromise between the two in terms of risk but requires an ongoing commitment to build business relationships.

TABLE 2 **STREAM CHECKLIST**

	Product development stream	**Content-driven stream**	**Affiliate network stream**
Market research	✓	✓	✓
Testing a product	✓		
Web design	✓	✓	✓
Sales letter synopsis	✓		
Product/information creation	✓		✓
Pay per click (PPC)	✓		✓
Search engine optimization (SEO)	✓	✓	✓
Article marketing	✓	✓	✓
Affiliate marketing	✓	✓	✓
Video marketing	✓	✓	✓
Split testing	✓		Optional
Advertise on your site	Optional	✓	✓

My first stream was product development, and remains my favorite method of creating income online. I love creating new products and the excitement of marketing them. For others, the slow and steady approach of content-rich sites appeals to their 'tortoise vs. hare' mentality, and rightfully so: their websites are a solid, risk-free foundation on which they can build a business that will last for years. Others still enjoy the personal element and create affiliate networks based on relationships built over time.

Now that we have introduced the three money-making streams and their associated personality types, it's time to explore their inner workings. Mastery of these topics will provide the backbone of your future online empire, funding adventures across the globe from Argentina to Zimbabwe. My advice is to focus on those most closely associated with your chosen stream first – this will help you get your stream up and running ASAP. However, before you build a stream, you must conduct thorough market research.

MARKET RESEARCH

Market research is the process of systematically collecting, recording and analyzing data about customers, competitors and the overall market. Using market research is a critical factor in the success of any stream. It can help you:

- create a business plan;
- launch a new product or service;
- improve existing products or services;
- expand into new markets.

Before you even think about creating a product to sell online, you need to ensure there is a demand for it. Here's how to conduct market research.

Find a niche market

The Internet has been around for a lot longer than most people realize, and many markets have already become saturated. Starting out, your best strategy is to focus on a niche market – a small specialized market within a larger market. For example, if you are interested in books, don't focus on the overall book market, focus on eighteenth-century English poetry, self-help with alcoholism, SAT prep tests, etc. Don't be a little fish in a big pond … be one of the few fish in a small pond.

Solutions sell

Darcie and I have developed numerous streams, each contributing a modest income. Some are mere trickles, others a steady flow. The main difference is that while all provide information to the visitor, our biggest earners provide solutions. Rather than brainstorming ideas for a product, find a common problem and offer a solution. For example, you can create a website that sells products for left-handed people (like Ned Flanders' Leftatorium).

Here's a list of where to find common markets, problems and ailments:

- **AquariumFish** lists their most popular articles.
- **Golf Online** is the place to check out if you're thinking about selling golf equipment.
- **The National Center for Infectious Diseases** is a site for people looking for a cure.
- **Consumer Reports Webwatch** is a goldmine for reviewing the top products that sell.
- **The Motley Fool** discusses finances and investing; it also lists its most popular articles.
- **Stockpickr!** is another investment site that lists its most popular pages.
- **CureZone** carries more health-related information.
- **Wedding Wisdom** covers weddings and relationship information.
- **Big Boards** lists all the big online forums, showing both the number of posts and members.

Criteria for a good online product

Bear in mind that some products sell better online than others. Here are the criteria I use for creating a solid product.

The product ...

- **has a low start-up cost.** You don't want to break the bank creating 10,000 copies of a product no one wants. My advice is stick to information-based products, which have limited products and are therefore the cheapest to start.
- **can be automated and is downloadable.** In order to automate your stream, you have to entirely remove yourself from the process. The more automated your stream is, the more scalable it becomes, allowing you to make more money while doing less work. While it is

possible to automate any business – from creating a product to selling a service – selling a downloadable product is the fastest route.

- **is digital.** From my experience, the best option for selling a product online is a digital product. A digital product is anything that can be sold as a download such as online books, music files, videos, information, etc.
- **provides a solution rather than just information.** Contrary to popular belief, most people don't buy e-books for information; they buy them because they need a solution. This applies to the size of the product as well; if you write a five-page e-book that includes step-by-step instructions on how to solve a common problem, someone will buy it.
- **can be expanded for up-selling and repeat business.** If your core product sells well, you'll make even more by offering your customers a platinum version and/or a paid subscription to your members-only newsletter.
- **can be advertised on other sites and vice versa (affiliates).** There are probably several other websites in your niche; you should build solid business relationships where you promote each other's products and services that are complementary, not competitive.

Market trends

There's an old saying 'A rising tide lifts all boats.' The opposite is also true: if you create your stream based on a topic with decreasing interest (such as VCR maintenance, MC Hammer albums, or Polaroid cameras) your profits will be washed out with the tide.

Before you choose a market, you should determine its long-term trend. A market trend shows how a market performed in the past, giving you an idea of its likely trend for the future. You should focus on long-term markets with a positive (increased interest over time) or level trend as they are more stable and will have a longer life span, rather than flavor-of-the-month topics. I can't imagine many authors of VCR manuals are still making royalties, though investment books pay dividends for decades. Stick with perennial topics and you'll receive many more paychecks in the future.

As you can see in Fig. 2, the Google Trends tool shows the average search volume for the term 'weight loss.' There's a consistent interest in weight loss topics over the past several years – a solid indication you could make money in this market for years to come. Notice how interest spikes every January?

FIGURE 2 **GOOGLE TRENDS FOR WEIGHT LOSS**

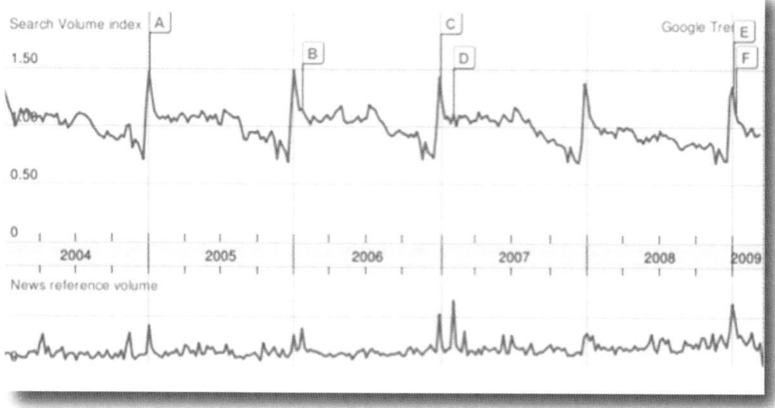

Trend tools

To determine the trending of your market, check out the following tools:

- **Google Trends** (www.google.com/trends) presents most popular current searches and allows you to analyze market stability and saturation.
- **Lycos 50** (www.lycos.com) offers a weekly list of the top pop culture searches on the web.
- **Yahoo Buzz** (www.buzz.yahoo.com) provides information on the top searches, commentary, and context.

- **Nielsen NetRatings** (www.nielsen-online.com) delivers comprehensive, independent measurement and analysis of online audiences.
- **TrendWatching** (http://trendwatching.com) is an independent and opinionated trend firm, scanning the globe for the most promising consumer trends, insights, and related hands-on business ideas.

Evaluate the demand

Now that you have found a niche market with a positive or level trend over the past few years, the next step is to determine the market size. Keep in mind that bigger is not necessarily better, but you still need a sizable pool of prospects if you intend to make money.

To determine the size of a market online, you need to discover what people are searching for as well as the terms they use. These terms are known as keywords, and keyword research is the foundation of market research.

Keyword research tools

- **Word Tracker** (www.WordTracker.com) helps you find what keywords and terms your market is searching for. This will help you with pay-per-click advertising and is essential for search engine optimization (SEO).
- **Trellian** (www.Trellian.com) is similar to WordTracker and helps you view filtered or non-filtered searches to see what other people are looking for.

These tools are necessary if you intend to market your site using SEO. However – and this is something no one ever mentions – ***if you advertise with PPC, the number of searches for a given keyword constitutes a very small part of your advertising efforts.*** More on this later.

You should also ask yourself whether people in this market are 'hunters' or 'gatherers.' Where gatherers are seeking information – say 'how to tie a tie' – they aren't likely to purchase anything. Hunters, on the other hand, are looking to buy a solution to their problem – 'teach me how to sing' or 'natural acne treatment' are two great examples of a buyer mentality.

THE LAW OF DEMAND AND SUPPLY

Everyone knows the law of supply and demand: when supply exceeds demand, prices drop; when demand exceeds supply, prices rise. Unfortunately, many misinterpret this when creating their streams. They focus on *supplying* a product, then look for a *demand*.

This is backwards thinking that will cause years of frustration. To ensure success in your streams, you need to focus on demand, which is why I refer to it as the *law of demand and supply*. Find a market that demands a solution, *then* supply it.

This shift in thinking has changed how I look at keyword research. Now I'll fire up WordTracker and enter keywords related to topics I enjoy reading (and writing) about. After scanning several underserved phrases, I'll check for synonyms, keeping an eye out for what I refer to as 'buying phrases.' These are terms such as 'hire copywriter' or 'purchase Canon digital camera' as opposed to information-gathering terms such as 'online copywriters' or 'how a digital camera works.' Once a demand has been confirmed, I'll start thinking how to supply a product.

Research the competition

Once you have determined a demand in your market, you'll need to research the competition. Remember how I said it's better to be one of the few fish in a small pond, not the only fish? Chances are, if you're attempting to enter a market that has zero competition, it's not a buying market. On the reverse side, you might not want to enter a market with multiple competitors – at least not until you sharpen your marketing skills.

So what exactly is your competition? Well, it depends on your marketing efforts. If you intend to market your website by paying for advertising, your competition would be those listed under 'Sponsored Links' on Google (Fig. 3), also known as AdWords. We'll cover paid advertising later in the pay-per-click section.

FIGURE 3 **GOOGLE SCREENSHOT OF COMPETITION PAYING FOR ADVERTISING**

If you are going to market your website without paying for advertising, also known as search engine optimization, your competition is the number of websites that appear for your keyword in quotes. For example, if you are optimizing your site for the phrase 'natural weight loss diet' you would search for that exact phrase in quotes:

'natural weight loss diet' NOT natural weight loss diet

The quotes show results for web pages that have that exact phrase at least once on their page (Fig. 4). Any phrase with less than 5,000 competing sites is fair game. In my experience, it is much harder to compete with more than 5,000 websites.

You can see from the screenshot there are more than 40,000 websites optimized for the phrase 'natural weight loss diet,' which is well above our 5,000 threshold. If you're serious about this market, you may still be interested.

FIGURE 4 **GOOGLE SCREENSHOT OF COMPETITION NOT PAYING FOR ADVERTISING**

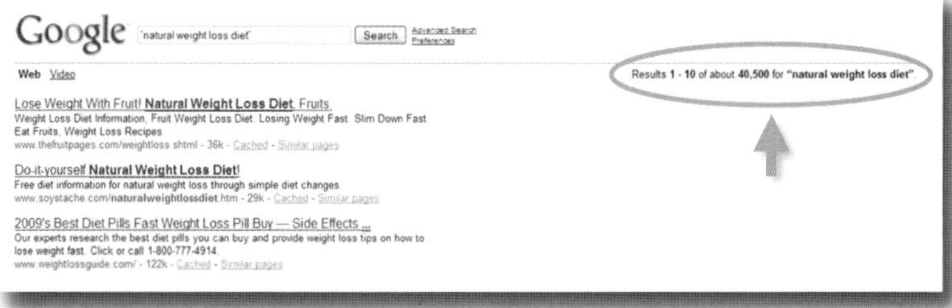

Once you've established the quantity of your competition, take a look at the first five web pages listed. You can see the first site has the title: 'Lose Weight With Fruit!' The website is about fruit, with a page dedicated to losing weight with a fruit diet. This is one angle.

The third site offers '2009's Best Diet Pills Fast Weight Loss Pill Buy …' Not exactly a catchy title, which leads me to believe they don't understand search engine optimization. (You'll be better off than them after reading the SEO section, I assure you.) Also, if someone is searching for natural weight loss diets, they probably aren't too interested in taking pills (unless they're all-natural supplements). I'm of the opinion that, even with a high number of competitors, you would be able to capture part of the market by releasing a Natural Weight Loss Diet Plan and Cookbook.

Scrutinize your top competitors and see if there is a place for you to shine. For example, are these sites well known in the diet industry? Do they use the term 'natural weight loss diet' in their headlines? Is it used several times throughout the text, or is it just mentioned in passing? What is their PageRank (see below)? Are there several other related pages on these websites (such as 'natural diet programs,' or 'natural diet pills'), or does this one page stray from the website's core topics (as seen in the fruit website)? These questions will help you determine how strong your competition is for the top spots and whether you can beat them at their own game. Check out www.stream-life.com for videos on effective keyword research.

PageRank (PR): it is … and isn't what you think

PageRank was created with the intent of measuring the relative importance of a site against all other sites on the Internet. This scale ranges from 0 to 10 and is logarithmic on a base of around 6. So, much like the Richter scale in measuring earthquakes, this means that a web page with a PR of 5 is six times more important than one with a PR of 4 (and so on up and down the scale), making a PR of 10 about six to the ninth power stronger than a PR 1, or about ten million times as strong. And because the scale is logarithmic it follows that a PR of 5.5 is nowhere near half way between a PR of 5 and a PR of 6.

As you can imagine, there are very few websites with a PR of 10 (Google and Adobe come to mind, while Yahoo! has a PR of 9).

A website's PageRank is determined by the quality of other websites linking to it. According to Wikipedia's PageRank diagram (see Fig. 5), Page C has a higher PageRank than Page E, even though it has fewer links to it. The one link it does have is from the highest valued website.

FIGURE 5 **PAGERANK DIAGRAM ON WIKIPEDIA**

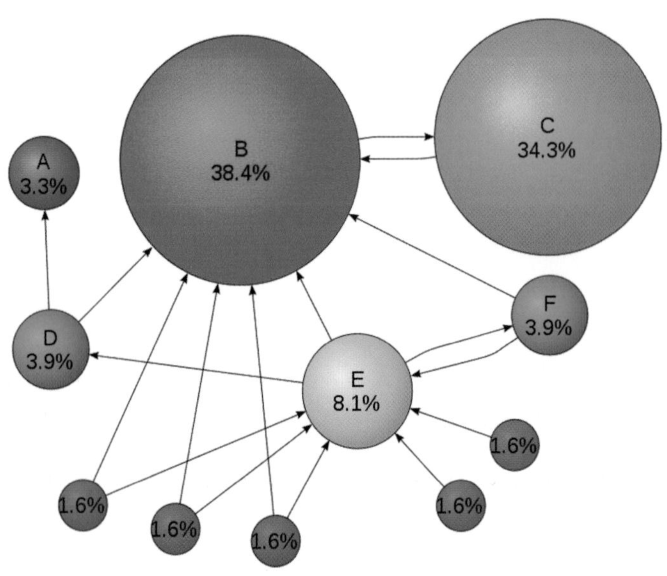

A website's highest PageRank is its home page, and decreases the further you navigate from there. If your home page carries a PR 6, any page one click away would be PR 5; two clicks away would fall to PR 4, etc.

Don't obsess over your own PR. In fact, Google only updates PR every three months, so you may not see any signs of improvement for some time. In addition, PR is really just a measuring stick to judge your competition. I've beaten a PR 6 site with a PR 0 site just by link-building and smart on-page optimization.

While Page Rank does in fact assign a rank to a web page, the term was coined in honor of its creator, Larry Page (co-founder of Google).

Competition research tools

- **Google Search Engine** (www.google.com). Google is the number one search engine out there, accounting for nearly 60% of all online searches. One of the best ways to analyze the competition is to see what your niche market is searching for and who the key players are.
- **Google AdWords Preview Tool** (https://AdWords.google.com/select/AdTargetingPreviewTool). With this tool you can search by country, domain, even a specific location for advertisements on Google without skewing the search results; you don't want 500 of the 550 daily searches for your phrase to be yours, right?
- **Quantcast** (www.quantcast.com). This website allows you to place HTML code on your website to gather demographic data about your market. To save time, enter your competition's URL into Quantcast and see who they're marketing to. Sometimes they won't cater to a demographic at all, giving you a strong advantage. Let's say you are selling ski equipment, and notice there is a market of older folks interested in snowboarding. You look at your competitors' sites and realize they are all aiming at the teenyboppers. You can differentiate yourself from the competition by marketing toward the underserved niche.

- **Google Toolbar** (www.google.com/tools/firefox/toolbar/FT5/intl/en/index.html – requires Firefox). With this tool, you can find a website's PageRank.

FIGURE 6 **GOOGLE TOOLBAR PAGERANK ICON**

General market research tools

- **SurveyMonkey** (www.surveymonkey.com) allows you to create your own customized online survey, and pick your prospects brains.
- **ClickZ** (www.clickz.com) provides columns with commentary and analysis on a wide variety of Internet marketing subjects ranging from business to business (B2B) marketing to search engine marketing.
- **FastCompany** (www.fastcompany.com) provides information on the economy and workplace for people who believe in performance with human values.
- **Pew Internet & American Life Project** (www.pewInternet.org) is a non-profit 'fact tank' that provides information on the issues, attitudes, and trends shaping America and the world.

Your approach to keywords will vary depending upon the number of searches and the competition. Always check the advertiser competition and the organic competition; you'll be amazed at the inconsistencies (see Fig. 9 below). I've seen popular phrases loaded with pay-per-click ads, with little to no SEO competition. The reverse is also true – for next to nothing in a click you can be on the first page of Google alongside highly optimized websites. Examine both the paid and organic results, and then choose the one that is less competitive.

Once your market research has convinced you to proceed, you'll want to test the demand for your product before creating it.

TEST YOUR PRODUCT

Product testing involves creating a website aimed to sell a product that hasn't been created yet, driving traffic to that website, and recording how many people complete a 'purchase.' Testing a product is the single most important part of market research because you can calculate the exact demand for your product before investing the resources to create it.

For the product development stream, there are three web pages you must create in order to test your product:

1. **Sales letter.** The first is a standard sales letter (covered in the section on sales page synopsis). Once someone reads the sales letter, they click on an Order Now button toward the bottom of the page.
2. **Order now.** On this page there is a summary of what the order will contain. A final order button is provided for the customer to continue with the purchase. Those who click this button are taken to the lead capture page.
3. **Lead capture page.** This page says 'We are currently updating our product, which will be re-launched very shortly. Please leave your name and e-mail address, and we'll notify you when it's ready.

Once you've created your three pages, create an AdWords campaign to drive traffic to your site and test whether or not your product will make you money.

Google Analytics code is added to each page, so you can track how far people get through your sales funnel. If you have several 'sales' and it looks like a winner, move ahead and create the product. If not, forget it and try something else.

AdWords and Google Analytics are discussed later in this book.

I tend to be pretty lenient when it comes to testing sales. I know that over time I'll improve our conversion rates through split testing ads, headlines, sales copy, etc. The important thing to find out is whether people are actually interested in buying the product. If I get a few nibbles, I'll proceed. Below we show you how to create a website not only to test a product but also to launch a real product when you're ready. You can also visit www.stream-life.com for videos on testing a product.

You can skip product testing with a content-driven or affiliate network stream.

WEBSITE DEVELOPMENT: CREATE A MONEY-MAKING WEBSITE

The good news is that you don't have to be a web developer to create a website. There are a number of web development tools and templates online that even the largest technophobes could handle. However, before we get into website development, you'll need a domain name and a host.

Domain names

A domain name is the name a visitor types into their URL address bar, such as yahoo.com, google.com, craigslist.org, youtube.com. First you'll need to register a domain name so no one else can use it. Choose a name that is descriptive of your business, catchy, and ideally has your main keywords in it.

In a perfect world, your domain name will be available on the first try, but chances are it won't. You can buy a domain name for one to five years and they typically range from $1.99 / £1.31 to $8.95 / £5.90 per year.

TRIVIA

Did you know that *.com* is for commercial businesses, *.net* is for networking organizations, and *.org* is for non-profit organizations? However, most websites typically use .com which has become the de facto standard. If you're dead set on a domain name but it's not available as a *.com*, try a different suffix.

Web hosting

Web hosting is when you pay a company to 'host' or store your website on their servers online. Basically, you'll create a website on your computer and upload the website to a web host, which puts it on the Internet (Fig. 7). Think of it like your e-mail provider. It's the same thing as creating a word document on your computer, attaching it to an e-mail and sending it to an identified recipient. Web hosts act the same way as the e-mail provider.

FIGURE 7 **WEB HOSTING AND DOMAIN NAME PROCESS FLOW**

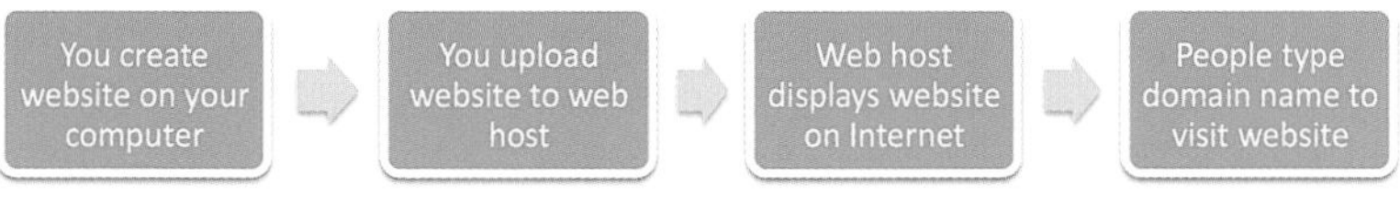

Hosting can range from nothing to $15 / £10 per month. Remember, you get what you pay for: many free web hosting packages put advertisements on your site. Space is also a concern: if your website is going to have a lot of graphics, flash animation (God forbid), audio, and content you might need to pay a little more for storage.

Most companies offer a domain name and web hosting as a package but you can transfer them as needed. I started with Yahoo! Small Business web hosting, but found their package and support horrible, not to mention expensive. After a few months, I opted to transfer my hosting to Blue Host and have been extremely happy with them ever since.

BLUE HOST – the best domain name and web hosting provider

Blue Host (www.BlueHost.com) is by far the best in the business …

- They are inexpensive at around \$7 / £4.50 a month for web hosting, plus \$10 / £6 a year for a domain name. (Bear in mind you probably won't be able to pay for the hosting monthly. They'll charge you for the entire year up front, but it's well worth it. You'll save a heap of cash in the long run.) The hosting fee covers unlimited domains, meaning that it gets cheaper with every stream you create.
- They have excellent support and customer service. After dealing with a few different web hosts, I got extremely frustrated with their lack of support. (To digress … I had a problem with my website and had to call Yahoo support four times in one week. Each time I called, I waited an average of one hour before reaching someone who gave me the runaround. That's when I opted to change to Blue Host.) Every time I've called Blue Host, they pick up the phone by the third ring and stay on the line until my questions are answered and my problems are solved. They are especially supportive of people who are new to setting up a website.
- They even accept calls from Skype (this is huge if you travel internationally).
- They have free e-mail accounts for your multiple businesses.

What else can I say? Feel free to browse around for another provider to see what's out there, but you'll be pleasantly satisfied if you choose Blue Host.

Website development tools

Once you've got your domain name and host, it's time to create your website. There are several web development tools available that can help.

I use Adobe's Dreamweaver because it's so user friendly you could probably teach yourself the basics in a few hours. It's a very popular application with tons of free YouTube demos on how to create a website.

The most current Dreamweaver software can be pricey, but if you buy an older version you're probably looking at about $50 / £30 to $100 / £60.

Alternatively, you could use XSitePro to help you create a professional website. It is a much cheaper option to Dreamweaver, and a hit among the technically disinclined.

If you're looking for a free version, check out NVU. It's the most popular free option on the market.

Website design

How you design your site will greatly affect its potential earnings. The primary rule when creating your website is to focus on simplicity. Most people get stuck at this stage trying to create a beautiful website with a fancy logo, flash navigation, modern layout, etc. Don't get distracted – your goal is to design a website that a three-year-old could navigate.

Depending upon which stream you choose, your website could have as few as three or as many as several hundred pages. Regardless of the number, keep your design simple. Here are some points to consider when creating your website:

1. **Provide good content.** Each page on your website should offer something of value. Don't let design get in the way of your content; every element on your web page – from a product image to the headline to the call to action – should elicit a specific response from your prospect. An opt-in page is designed to create leads. A sales page is meant to sell your product. A privacy policy should assure people you will not sell their information. And so on. Don't confuse your prospects with mixed messages; subtly guide them to each page's intended purpose.

2. **Avoid cheesy elements.** Design your website to look clean and professional. Try to avoid elements such as animation, blinking text, annoying sound effects, multiple colors, etc. because they will distract the visitor and potentially annoy them.

3. **Don't use pop-up windows.** Do you like visiting a website with pop-up windows? Me neither.

4. **Let your prospects know where they are.** You have about three seconds to grab a user's attention before they hit the Back button, so be strategic in your placement of information and images. According to the article 'Clarity trumps persuasion' by www.marketingexperiments.com, a visitor to your website needs to answer the following three questions within a few seconds:
   (a) 'Where am I?'
   (b) 'What can I do/get/buy here?'
   (c) 'Why should I participate?'

5. **Design for easy navigation.** Organize your content into a logical manner with one intended response for each page. Be sure to include a navigation menu near the top of every page so people can find it without scrolling to the bottom. Here is an example of what a navigation bar might contain:
   (a) Home Page / Sales Letter
   (b) Company Information
   (c) Products & Services
   (d) Ordering
   (e) Support
   (f) Contact

6. **Go home from every page.** Allow the user to get back to the home page from every page on your website. Put a 'home' link in the navigation bar to avoid this problem.

7. **Don't bury information.** It is annoying when it takes ten clicks to find what you're looking for – and most people won't try that hard. Never have web pages that go more than three clicks away from the home page.

8. **Use flash cautiously, if at all.** Flash and multimedia may add a nice visual touch to your web page, but if used poorly they can distract your visitors from finding the information they need. Web designers love to create flashy intros to websites. Not only does this fail to

provide any search engine optimization (SEO) benefit, it often frustrates your visitors. How many times have you clicked 'Skip Intro' when there is a flash video playing?

9. **Focus on website readability.** It is important to consider how the web design will affect the readability of the information.
   (a) Don't make your webpage wider than 800 pixels.
   (b) Don't make any line of text wider than 600 pixels.
   (c) Make the text large enough to read.
   (d) Increase line spacing.
   (e) Don't type more than a few words in ALL CAPS.
   (f) Don't use more than one exclamation point!
   (g) Use a spelling and grammar checker.

10. **Use proper link formatting.** There is a right and wrong way to use links. Be sure to do the following:
    (a) Don't underline words if they're not links.
    (b) Don't open internal links in a new window.
    (c) Use descriptive link text – especially keywords.
    (d) Test your links.

11. **Provide your contact info.** In order to build customer trust, you must be accessible if they have questions or concerns.

If you're having trouble getting started with web design, visit some of your favorite sites and note their design elements. Why reinvent the wheel and start designing from scratch when there are millions of websites to inspire you?

Web images

Images not only make your website more aesthetically pleasing, they can also communicate the content you have to offer. For example, if you put a product picture in the upper left corner of the sales page, you are sending a clear message to the visitor what you are selling.

So how do you get these wonderful images?

1. Use your **digital camera**. It is free, you control the images, and you don't have to worry about copyright issues.

2. **Flickr** (www.flickr.com) is an online photo management and sharing application that allows you to share and use photos. You can search for pictures that are licensed under Creative Commons license, allowing you to use their pictures, provided you link back to their gallery.

   You can also search for pictures that have been voted as the most interesting in their category. There are two ways to search for images you can reuse: on the Flickr site, click on advanced search and be sure to click the checkboxes at the bottom for Creative Commons licenses. If you use Firefox – and you should – type what you're looking for in the Creative Commons search engine located at the top right of your browser.

   For the definitive guide to using Flickr images, read the article on http://www.skelliewag.org.

3. **Product box images.** You can use these online services to help create e-book covers:
   - Free Tool: www.ebookcovercreator.com
   - Paid $27 / £18: www.ecovercreator.net

Adobe's Photoshop is a great image editing tool, but it's challenging to learn and may require taking a class or two.

SALES LETTER SYNOPSIS

A sales letter is the page designed to sell your product. You can have a fantastic product, but you won't earn anything if your sales letter lacks sizzle.

Your sales letter should grab a visitor's attention, prove that you provide a solution, remove risk, state a call to action, and (if done well) generate a sale (Fig. 8).

FIGURE 8 **SALES LETTER PROCESS FLOW**

All great sales letters include the following:

1. Catchy headers and subheaders
2. Unique selling proposition
3. Stated product benefits
4. Testimonials
5. Special offers
6. Digital covers
7. Video demos
8. Exceptional guarantees
9. Trust building techniques
10. Bonuses
11. Follow-ups
12. A PS

Catchy headers and subheaders

Your main header, also referred to as an H1 tag, can:

- Target a pain point: 'Are You Losing Your Hair?'
- Highlight a benefit: 'Now You Can Re-grow Your Hair … Without Chemicals!'
- Invoke curiosity: 'Can Broccoli Prevent Hair Loss?'
- Include keywords.

Your subheaders will follow the same format as your header. These two work best when they attack the reader from two different angles. Your headline could invoke curiosity, while the subheader makes a bold claim like this: 'Now You Can Re-grow Your Hair … Without Chemicals!'

EXAMPLE HEADLINES FOR A SALES LETTER

- Who Else Wants _______?
- The Secret of _________
- Here's How You Can [benefit] Without [problem] ...
- Little Known Ways to _____________
- Get Rid of _______________ Once And For All!
- WARNING: This Letter Is For Serious __________ Only.
- Are You Still Suffering From _________?
- Are You Making These Same Mistakes?
- At Last! The [credibility indicator like 'Bestselling' or 'As seen on Oprah'] Stream That Is Revolutionizing ___________
- Save Yourself 30% on _________ By Following These Simple Steps
- How I Went From [loser] to [winner] in Just 2 Weeks!
- How To [Cook Thai Food] Like The [Locals]
- 56 Ways ____________ Saves You Time, Work and Money

Highlight your unique selling proposition

This is where you subtly demonstrate to your reader that your competition sucks. To do this, examine your competitors' sales letters, noting the benefits they offer – and, more importantly, those they lack. Even if the two of you are selling the same product, you can position your offer in very different ways. Are they offering a money-back guarantee? Do they fail to cover a specific topic that you explain in detail? Discover your competitor's weaknesses and demonstrate them to your prospects ... Chances are, your prospects will shop around before committing, and it pays to plant the seeds of doubt in their minds about your competitors. Remember that subtlety is the key – you don't want to smear yourself as well!

Focus on benefits, not features

Don't rattle off the features of your product – explain to your prospect how they will benefit from it. For example, if you're selling air conditioners, people aren't interested in the features (e.g. voltage, wattage, what type of plastic it's made of, etc.): they want to keep cool during summer!

To ensure you're listing benefits instead of features, ask yourself 'How does this feature help my prospect?' List your features, then add the word 'which' after it: whatever follows is a benefit. For example:

- Low power requirements, which lowers your energy bill.
- New polymer plastic casing, which cools your house faster than traditional models.
- Timer setting, which saves you the hassle of getting up in the middle of the night to turn it off.

I've heard this phrase so many times I practically recite it in my sleep, yet so many people forget this simple law of copywriting. Bullet points tend to work best in sales letters, as they are easily scanned by readers. Keep in mind that your prospects aren't interested in every single benefit your product offers, just the ones that apply to them. By listing dozens of benefits, you are increasing the likelihood your prospects will come across one or two main benefits they are most interested in and buy your product.

Include testimonials

Darcie and I were on Ko Phi Phi Island in Thailand (where the movie The Beach was filmed) getting ready to grab a bite to eat. While looking at a map, a couple of guys came up to us and recommended a restaurant saying, 'This is the best restaurant we've been to on the island. You should check it out.'

Guess where we went for dinner?

We didn't personally know these guys, yet we trusted them. This demonstrates what is known as social proof – people making decisions based on someone else's experience. If you're interested in something and you see that it has worked for others, you are likely to trust them and buy the product. Testimonials are a great way to demonstrate social proof to your prospects; they can see for themselves that your product works and provides value to real people without you forcing it down their throats. Rather than singing your own praises, why not let your satisfied customers do it for you?

Here's two ways to gather testimonials.

1. When first testing your product (that is, the product you haven't created yet) ask people you know personally if they can provide testimonials citing your expertise in a specific area applicable to your product.
2. Once you create and sell your product, follow up with the customer via e-mail and ask for a testimonial. Here's what I use:

> Dear <first name of prospect>
>
> Thanks for taking our free course on <subject>. Many others have written to tell us how this course has helped <highlight main benefit>, and I sincerely hope you feel the same way.
>
> I'd like to ask a favor. We're always trying to improve our course, and would greatly appreciate your feedback. If it's OK with you, please take a moment and jot down your thoughts in the box below. I promise not to include any personal information other than your name and city.
>
> Feel free to say whatever you feel. If you have some ideas on how to improve our course, we're all ears.
>
> Thanks <first name of prospect>, and I hope to hear from you soon.
>
> Best regards,
>
> <your name> <your website> <your e-mail address>

Testimonial Box

I understand that <name of your company> has the right to use these comments in their marketing material. I also understand <name of your company> will NOT use any personal information with the exception of my name and city.

Comments:

Make sure to include a personal e-mail address you check frequently in order to stay on top of testimonials as they come in.

Some people recommend offering an incentive in exchange for a testimonial such as a free report, though I've never had any trouble securing them with this form. Besides, if your free course isn't good enough to warrant praise, you probably need to reconsider your product offer.

As the testimonials start to roll in, put them on your sales page.

People don't buy products ... they buy offers

You may have the single greatest product in the history of humanity, guaranteed to cure a wide variety of ailments, train your dog to stop barking and initiate world peace, but without compiling it into a dynamite offer your product will fall flatter than a soufflé in a snowstorm.

Think of it this way: when you go to a fine dining restaurant, you're not just paying for the flavor of the food; you're also paying for the presentation. Your offer is the presentation; if your prospects don't like the presentation they won't even try your product. This is why creating a solid offer is imperative for your stream's success.

So what makes a good offer? Below are the key components.

Have a quality digital cover

If you're creating an information product that includes several downloadable CDs, create a professional looking digital CD cover for each disc. If you have an e-book or special report, create covers for those as well. Be sure to include screenshots of the content as well, which should be professionally formatted.

Include video demos

Videos are a great tool for marketing your product and should be used wherever possible – I've used video demos for several products with great success. The process is simple: use Camtasia to record you demonstrating your product while explaining its benefits, then upload the video to YouTube and embed the code they give you onto your website. We'll talk about video marketing more in a bit.

Offer an exceptional guarantee

The main function of a guarantee is to remove all risk for your prospect. You want to make a guarantee so strong they'd feel like a fool for not buying your product. For example, you could offer a 60-day money-back guarantee, and allow them to keep all the bonuses even if they decide to cancel. Another method is to allow your prospect to download your product for one dollar, and then charge their credit card the remainder seven days later if they don't cancel.

Build trust

When I receive e-mails from people asking me 'Is this for real?' I know it's time to build a higher level of trust with our prospects. Be sure to include links to your privacy policy, contact information and a brief bio about yourself.

Privacy policy

Your privacy policy should go something like this:

<Your Business Name>: Privacy Policy

<Your Business Name> is committed to protecting the privacy and security of individuals that have contacted us. It is with that purpose in mind that we have formed our privacy guarantee. We realize that the concerns you bring to us are highly personal in nature. We assure you that all information shared will be managed within legal and ethical considerations.

Security of Information

We restrict access to personal information to employees who have a specific business purpose in utilizing your data. Our employees are trained in the importance of maintaining confidentiality and member privacy.

Accuracy of Information

We strive to ensure that our records contain accurate information. If there are any changes to your contact information (e.g. phone number, e-mail, etc.), please e-mail <your e-mail address>. We will promptly make any necessary changes to update your records.

Changes to Our Guarantee

We reserve the right to revise our privacy guarantee as our business needs change or as the law requires. If we revise our policy, we will provide you with the new policy at that time.

Web Links to Other Websites

Links to third-party sites may be available from 'www.yourwebsite.com.' Sites outside the 'www.yourwebsite.com' domain are NOT maintained by <Your Business Name> and <Your Business Name> is NOT responsible for the content or availability of linked sites. Recommended links are NOT an endorsement or guarantee of other sites or organizations and are simply provided for reference. The privacy and security policies of linked sites are likely to differ from <Your Business Name> and users are encouraged to review the privacy and security policies of these sites.

Contact information

Get a PO box at your local post office and use that as your mailing address. This will provide you with peace of mind – you don't want your home address advertised to hundreds of thousands of people, right?

It's always better to include a phone number as well. You can leave your personal number, or get a redirect line through Skype or Vonage. If you receive lot of calls, consider signing up with a call center that will take messages and accept payments (there's a list of them at the end of this book).

Bio

Including a bio is a great opportunity for you to sell yourself and build trust with readers, many of whom want to know a little about a person before doing business with them. Bios typically include the following elements:

- educational background
- professional background
- experience with current business/product
- special achievements
- personal information (e.g. city of residence and family information)
- picture.

All of these are completely optional and depend on how comfortable you feel with sharing information online. There is a fine line between highlighting your knowledge, skills, and achievements and coming across as a show-off. Remember: the point is to build trust, hopefully to the point of getting a sale.

Offer bonuses

Once you've demonstrated that your product provides value and removed risk with a strong guarantee, push your prospects off the fence with a few value-packed bonuses. The bonus is all about perceived value – many people in fact buy products for the bonuses themselves! If you're offering an e-book on Cajun cooking, offer a video that demonstrates how to make roux and several Cajun sauces. How about recipes for cocktails that are famous in the South? A list of the best restaurants in New Orleans? All of these are easy to create and dramatically improve the value of your product.

Follow-up

Let's say your prospects sign up for a free two-week course on Southern cooking. They are then presented with an offer to buy the full product. If they haven't purchased it, they receive another e-mail, but with a twist: this could be a reduced price, an added bonus, or the chance to pay in installments.

State a PS

Believe it or not, many people will scroll to the bottom of a sales page first. I do it all the time ... once I know I'm on a sales page, the first question that comes to mind is 'How much?'

This is precisely why you shouldn't list your price at the bottom of your sales letter. Instead, use a PS, or just another headline that reinforces your value proposition. Rather than asking 'How much?' they'll scroll up to learn more about your offer.

HOW TO WRITE SALES LETTERS

To learn how to write a great sales letter, visit the Michel Fortin blog (http://www.michelfortin.com/) and click on some of the products he markets. (Michel Fortin has sold more products than anyone on the web, and his copywriting skills are legendary ... seriously.)

I strongly suggest you read The Ultimate Sales Letter by Dan S. Kennedy. If you can't stand the idea of creating them, check out Yanik Silver's Instant Sales Letters (http://www.instantsalesletters.com/), where you just fill in the blanks – you can have a sales letter up and running within five minutes. I've used several of them in the past, and they convert visitors to buyers really well for niches targeting business people. However, if you target other markets that don't include business owners or professionals, they tend to convert poorly.

PRODUCT CREATION

If your test proved a winner, it's time to start creating the product. If you want full control of creating your product, by all means do it yourself. However, if you're strapped for time, consider outsourcing the product creation and website development. Before you begin, have a clear product outline, including bonuses.

There are several ways to add value to your product. You can record an interview with an expert in your niche and incorporate that into your product ... Take a look at CNet (www.cnet.com) for software that may be reused for commercial purposes ... Go on a related forum and ask people what they'd most like to learn about ... All of these should help get the juices flowing. If you're still struggling with creating the product, there is a treasure trove of information within the public domain.

PUBLIC DOMAIN

While we usually create our own products and books, you can save a lot of time using material that is in the public domain. The public domain can be considered the anti-copyright: you can use any book, image, or audio for whatever purpose you see fit. You can even take a book and resell it without making a single change. Items in the public domain don't belong to somebody, they belong to everybody.

Don't believe the hype from people who want to sell you access to public domain material; by law, everyone has access to this service. Here are a few resources to get you going:

- www.banis-associates.com/pdlist/ – PD links
- www.gutenberg.org/ – lots of books in txt format
- www.gpoaccess.gov/advancedsearch.html – search for US government documents (state documents are not in the public domain, just federal)
- http://digital.library.upenn.edu/books/ – PD books
- www.booksforabuck.com/general/pubsources.html
- www.copyright.gov/records/cohm.html – copyright search

ACCEPT ONLINE PAYMENTS

Accepting payments online is the next step to business automation. Online payments are where a user makes a payment for a product or service online rather than in person or through the mail. It's fast, easy, hassle free, and secure. One of the best ways to build a visitor's trust is to use a secure payment processor such as PayPal.

I typically work with PayPal because they are one of the most widely used online payment providers, and well regarded for their security. You can accept payments and make payments with them with a click of a button.

In order to set up this process, all you have to do is:

- Create a business account with PayPal.
- Connect the PayPal account to your business checking account so you can deposit the money you accept online.
- Create a 'Buy Now' button code – simply enter the product name and amount and the code will be generated.
- Put the 'Buy Now' button code on your webpage.

When users visit your website, they:

- Click the 'Buy Now' button that you put on your website and are directed to a PayPal page where they see the product name and amount.
- Enter their PayPal account or credit card information to purchase.
- Are given a summary of their purchase, and receive an e-mail confirmation from PayPal.

You will also be sent an e-mail notification that you've made a sale. Honestly, seeing these notifications in my Inbox is a constant reminder that my streams are a success.

Another great feature of PayPal is that you are only charged a percentage of the overall sales amount plus a small transaction fee. This means you're not out of pocket until someone buys. Also, if for some reason a buyer wanted to return a product, issuing a refund is as simple as logging into your account, finding the transaction, and clicking a button. They also offer a variety of reporting tools to help you track overall sales figures for monthly totals and taxes.

Payment processors

- **PayPal** (www.PayPal.com)
- **ClickBank** (www.ClickBank.net)
- **Google Checkout** (http://checkout.google.com/): they don't charge a transaction fee if you use AdWords.

I suggest offering multiple payment processors on your website in case a visitor doesn't feel comfortable with one.

DELIVER DIGITAL PRODUCTS

The easiest method for delivering digital products is E-Junkie (http://www.e-junkie.com) which will process and deliver all your digital products for $5 / £3.30 a month. It is compatible with PayPal, ClickBank, 2CheckOut, and Google Checkout. All you have to do is upload your product to their website, link E-Junkie with your payment processor account information (e.g. PayPal) and E-Junkie will do the rest. They even manage an affiliate program for you as well, for no added cost. They have excellent customer service and an easy-to-use interface. Can you tell I like these guys or what?

After a user purchases your product through PayPal, they will automatically be redirected to a page on E-Junkie (which you can customize) with a link to download your product. As a backup, they also send the user an e-mail with the download link in case they didn't get redirected. It's a completely automated process and is simple to use.

You can watch a video on setting up PayPal and E-Junkie on your site at www.stream-life.com.

ADVERTISE ON YOUR SITE

Once you have your website up and running, you can make additional revenue by placing advertisements for other people's products/services on it. This is remarkably simple. There are three main ways you can accept advertising, discussed below from easiest to implement to hardest.

Google AdSense

With Google AdSense you display Google ads on your website and get a commission when someone clicks on those ads. This is the simplest way to generate income from advertising on your website. Sign up for a Google AdSense (www.google.com/adsense) account, determine how you want the ads to display (vertical, horizontal, etc.) and place the Google-generated code onto your website. Google analyzes the web page and provides ads that are contextually related to your content. For example, if your website is about snow skis, Google provides ads about snow skis. You (as the website owner) get paid whenever someone clicks on those ads.

At least, that's the idea. First, there has to be people paying to advertise for snow skis. Second, Google has to accurately read your webpage to provide the right ads: it's possible to have ads for water skis show up on your page, which is of no benefit to anyone.

Most people using AdSense make a few cents to a few dollars a day, though large websites can earn several hundred to a thousand dollars a day. The name of the game is traffic: the more traffic that visits your site and the more people click on the ads, the more you get paid.

By the way, don't think Google can't tell if you're clicking your own ads – they can, and will revoke your account!

Affiliate advertising

Affiliate advertising is similar to Google AdSense, but in this case an advertiser places an ad on your website and you receive a commission if the prospect goes on to purchase their product. You can advertise other people's products on your website and advertise your products on other websites. This is further explained in the section on affiliate marketing.

If you want to place an affiliate ad on your site, visit their website and see if they have any promotional ads you can use. Many sales letters have a link at the bottom for affiliates, and provide the code for you. While AdSense makes you cents every day, these ads will pay you dollars only when a sale is made – which might take some time.

Charge by impression

This method is more in tune with traditional advertising like in a newspaper. Let's say your website receives 10,000 views – known as impressions – per month: you can charge advertisers $2 / £1.32 per thousand impressions, meaning you earn $20 / £13.20 per advertiser per month – even if no sales are made. This takes a little more time to set up because you'll need to initiate and actively maintain relationships with advertisers.

PRODUCT LAUNCH CHECKLIST

Before launching a product, you'll want to use the final checklist shown in Table 3, organized by stream.

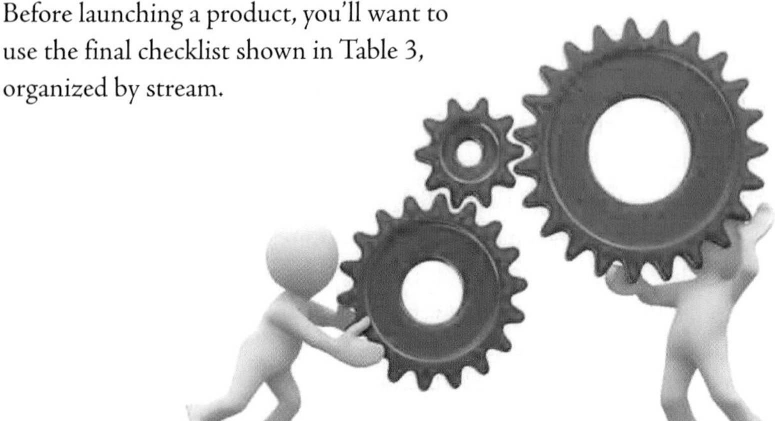

TABLE 3 **PRODUCT LAUNCH CHECKLIST**

	Product development stream	Content-driven stream	Affiliate network stream
Add Google Analytics code to all pages	✓	✓	✓
Add your IP address as a filter for Google Analytics (www.whatismyipaddress.com)	✓		✓
Set up goals in Google Analytics	✓		
Add Quantcast code	✓	✓	✓
Add and test AdSense code	✓ Optional	✓	✓ Optional
Add Google AdWords conversion code to key pages	✓		✓ Mandatory, with AdWords
Check that website displays properly in Explorer and Firefox	✓	✓	✓
Check website links	✓	✓	✓
Test autoresponder	✓	✓ Optional	✓
Test payment processing	✓		✓
Test digital download delivery	✓		✓
Test e-mail address	✓	✓	✓
Test videos			

DRIVE TRAFFIC TO YOUR WEBSITE

Now that you've developed a product, it's time to drive as many qualified prospects to your website as possible. A common misconception is that more traffic is better than less traffic, when in fact the opposite is true: you only want traffic that converts by signing up for a newsletter or buying a product.

For example, let's look at two websites.

1. **Website 1:** receives 1,000 visitors per day, and manages to sell one product totaling $100 / £65 in revenue.
2. **Website 2:** receives a paltry 10 visitors per day, but since the traffic is highly qualified, they manage to sell two products totaling $200 / £130 in revenue.

Which site would you rather have?

Of course, this doesn't factor in advertising costs; it depends on whether you are paying for that traffic or not.

1. Website 1: gets 1,000 visitors per day from sources such as search engine optimization and article marketing, without paying a penny for advertising. Their profit is essentially $100 / £65 per day.
2. Website 2: gets 10 visitors, but spends $150 / £100 in advertising – a painful yet plausible expense for hyper-competitive markets. Their profit drops to $50 / £35 a day.

Let's take a look at how you can drive visitors to your website. The three main methods of generating traffic are:

1. pay-per-click (PPC)
2. search engine optimization (SEO)
3. article marketing.

As you can see from Table 4, each method has its advantages. In order to test a product you should use PPC for its speed and ability to split test. Once you've split test a number of ads/offers, you'll have a much better idea what your market is looking for and should proceed to develop an effective SEO campaign, which should include article marketing to a certain extent. Let's take a look at each method in greater detail, starting with pay-per-click advertising.

TABLE 2 **TRAFFIC SUMMARY**

	PPC	SEO	Article marketing
Free traffic		✓	✓
Immediate traffic	✓		✓
Easily tested	✓		
Long-term traffic	✓	✓	Decrease over time

Pay-per-click (PPC)

Advertising used to be a risky venture. You paid for a TV spot, billboard, or radio ad aimed at an assumed targeted market and prayed. Nowadays, it's much easier and more cost-effective.

Thanks to the Internet, you can now market directly to people interested in your product. Rather than throwing your ads on the wall and seeing what sticks, you now have laser-beam focus with pay-per-click advertising.

FIGURE 9 **GOOGLE PPC AND ORGANIC SEARCH RESULTS**

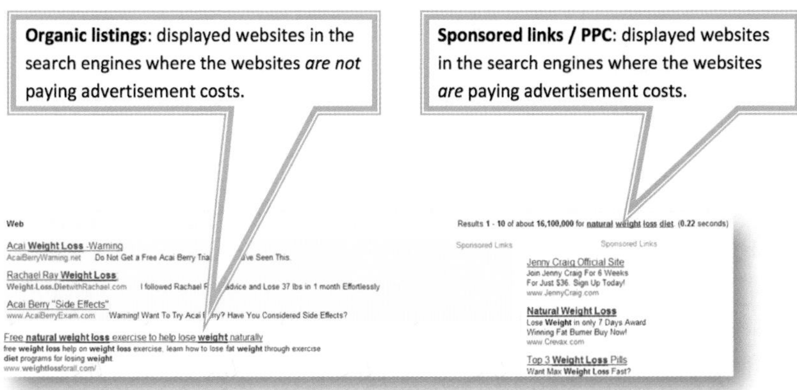

Pay-per-click (PPC) is a form of online advertising where a business only pays when a person clicks on their ad. A business will determine all the relevant keywords for a product, write an ad for those keywords, and place bids with search engines (such as Google) to have their ads show up in their results for those keywords. For example, if someone searches for the keyword 'weight loss', by using PPC, a business website will be listed alongside the search engine results. Figure 9 displays a Google search with both the natural search results (also known as 'organic') and PPC, listed under 'Sponsored Links.'

Google AdWords

A paradigm shift in advertising occurred with the emergence of Google's pay-per-click model called AdWords. Rather than have the top spot on Google solely dependent on the amount you bid, Google rewards you for relevancy.

How AdWords works is shown in Fig. 10. The higher both of the numbers on the left, the higher your position. For example, let's say two people bid $1 / £0.66 to have their ad appear for the term 'fried chicken recipes.' Advertiser A creates a highly relevant ad for fried chicken recipes; Advertiser B creates an ad for chicken farms.

FIGURE 10 **GOOGLE ADWORDS EQUATION**

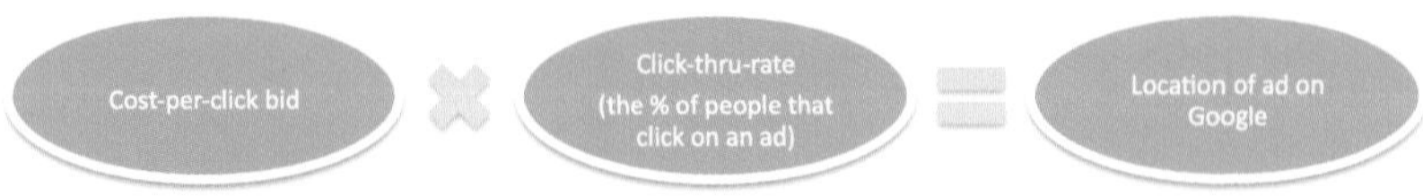

Guess which one more people clicked on?

At the end of the week Advertiser A had a click-through-rate (CTR) of 2%, while Advertiser B had a CTR of 1% (perhaps a lot of people are interested in chicken farms). This is where the genius of AdWords comes in: because Advertiser A gets twice as many clicks, they will actually pay less per click than Advertiser B and be placed on top. This can be a vicious cycle for Advertiser B because they will not have the same level of exposure as Advertiser A, resulting in even fewer clicks and higher costs.

How can Advertiser B get out of this downturn? Simple: rewrite their ad so it focuses more readily on fried chicken recipes. Once they do that, more people will respond to the ad by clicking on it, and their ad costs will go down (due to their higher relevance) while their clicks increase.

The relevancy of your ad will improve your CTR, though you can also buy your way to the top. In the previous example, both websites bid the same amount. If Advertiser B bid $2 / £1.30 per click, they may have been placed at the top of the search results initially; however, the relevancy laws would have eventually increased their cost-per-click and dragged them down.

Bear in mind that you could theoretically write a completely unrelated ad that will result in more clicks ('Improve Your Sex Life!'), but you will not profit from it for two reasons:

1. Someone who clicks on that ad is not really interested in fried chicken recipes at the moment, and is less likely to buy from you.
2. Secondly, Google will realize the ruse and punish you.

By creating an ad that is obviously off topic, Google will raise your minimum bid, sometimes as high as $10 / £6. Within a short while, your credit card burning, you will take down the ad or at least attempt to make it relevant ('Improve Your Sex Life With Fried Chicken!').

I could write hundreds of pages on how to set up AdWords, but Google does a pretty good job in their training center. (I should know, I had to read the whole damn thing twice before taking their professionals exam.) You'll get the gist of it at the Google Training Center.

However, Google does not mention this, and it's important before you begin. You should always set up three campaigns in AdWords for each of the following (and maybe more in the future).

1. **Campaign C:** this is for ads showing on the Google content network. (These are not triggered by searches, but rather are placed conceptually on a webpage. For example, Google looks at our ad group for seminar marketing, and will place that ad on websites about seminars, marketing, etc.)
2. **Campaign G:** this is for ads that appear on Google.com only, and is based on keywords. So if someone types in 'seminar marketing' it will show on Google.
3. **Campaign S:** this is for ads that appear on the Google search network (such as Ask.com, Myspace.com, etc.), and are based on keywords. For example, if someone goes to Myspace.com and searches for 'seminar marketing' our ad will show on their results page.

Why do this? Many people create only one campaign, which is a flawed tactic. With just one campaign, Google mixes all the data together, so you can't tell at a glance if you're doing better on the search network or the content network. With three campaigns we know on the very first page how much we are spending on each source, and how well they are converting (Fig. 11). Much cleaner.

FIGURE 11 **GOOGLE ADWORDS CAMPAIGNS**

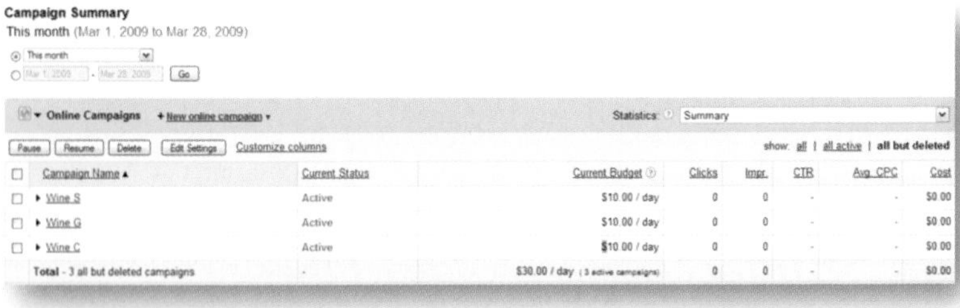

Campaign Summary
This month (Mar 1, 2009 to Mar 28, 2009)

Online Campaigns + New online campaign — Statistics: Summary

Pause | Resume | Delete | Edit Settings | Customize columns — show: all | all active | all but deleted

Campaign Name	Current Status	Current Budget	Clicks	Impr.	CTR	Avg. CPC	Cost
Wine S	Active	$10.00 / day	0	0	-	-	$0.00
Wine G	Active	$10.00 / day	0	0	-	-	$0.00
Wine C	Active	$10.00 / day	0	0	-	-	$0.00
Total - 3 all but deleted campaigns	-	$30.00 / day (3 active campaigns)	0	0	-	-	$0.00

When you create a new campaign Google will ask you where you want it displayed: the search and/or content networks. The problem is they won't let you select the search network without the Google network, meaning you Campaign G and Campaign S will overlap.

Here's what you do: select the search network for both campaigns, but set Campaign S's maximum bid five to ten cents less than Campaign G. This way, Campaign G shows up for Google (due to the higher bid) and Campaign S shows up everywhere else.

I could take several paragraphs describing the account setup, but you'll get the gist of it at the Google Training Center. Visit www.stream-life.com for a video on how I set up my AdWords campaigns.

AdWords advice

Here are some additional pointers that will help you get your AdWords campaigns running smoothly:

- **Run for the border.** If you're attempting to advertise in a highly competitive market, don't advertise in the United States at first. Other English-speaking countries such as England, Australia, Canada, Ireland, and New Zealand are often less competitive which allows you a smaller arena in which to sharpen your skills. Additionally, it will lower your overall ad spend. How? Google factors in your account performance history when determining your bid price; if you achieve a high click-through-rate in other countries, your bid price will be lower when you do decide to advertise in the United States.
- **Bid high at first.** For the reason listed above, it's important to have a strong performance history. Therefore you should plan to bid higher on your keywords initially in order to appear higher in the search results (thereby improving your click-through-rate), and then lower your bids over time.
- **Use robots to block search engines.** Search engines crawl your website in order to understand its purpose. Analytics will record some of these visits, which you may misinterpret as a potential sale. For example, if you're testing a new product and you want to see how many people reach an 'Order Now' page, there may have only been three humans who visited the page but also ten robots. You would mistakenly conclude there were 13 sales when in fact there were only

three. In order to prevent this create a robots.txt file. This tells the search engines not to crawl a specific page, and helps keep your data consistent. Admittedly, this is an extreme example, but something to consider.

- **Use AdWords Editor.** Once you're on the road, you'll find Internet access to be costly and/or difficult. With the Editor, you can make changes to your account offline, and then upload the changes when you have access. In addition, AdWords Editor allows you to copy changes made in one campaign and paste them into another; this alone saves hours of work!
- **Bid on common misspellings.** These terms tend to be much cheaper to bid on, and the competition is greatly reduced.
- **Learn from your competitors' mistakes.** You can reap a lot of great information from your AdWords competition before moving online. Using Keyword Spy's Time Machine, you can see ads your competitors have used in the past (obviously the ones they don't use anymore didn't work for them, and probably won't work for you). Their current winners can point you in the right direction for your new campaign. Are they asking a question in their headline? Do they include the keyword in the ad text? Do they highlight a pain point? Offer a solution? Learn from their mistakes (i.e. identify why certain angles don't work) and get your campaign off to a flying start.
- **Use the Ad Preview Tool.** If you want to preview your AdWords but don't want to accrue impressions, use Google's AdWords Preview Tool. It also allows you to search by country, region, and language. Want to see what your ads look like in Thailand? Now you can.

In order to run a profitable AdWords campaign, the key is relevance. We want someone who types in 'Learn Spanish' to click on our ad which says 'Learn Spanish Now!' and is directed to a landing page that promotes Spanish classes only.

Think of your sales process like a hallway. You want your prospects to open a door (click your ad), walk down the hall (learn about the course), and walk out the door at the end of the hall (pay for a course). Anything that does not explicitly help this process (Italian classes, links to other sites, directory links, etc.) is like adding more doors to the hallway. This gives your prospect a chance to head in a direction away from a sale.

If there is one thing I cannot stress enough, it's this: profit follows relevance.

AdWords Tools

- Google AdWords (http://adwords.google.com)
- Google AdWords Training Center (www.google.com/adwords/learningcenter/)
- Google AdWords Editor (www.google.com/intl/en/adwordseditor/)
- Google Ad Preview Tool (https://AdWords.google.com/select/AdTargetingPreviewTool)

So how do you measure what's working and what not? This is where conversion tracking comes in.

Conversion tracking

You're over the moon. You have just created a campaign with ten ad groups and are already turning a profit. However, you're not sure which ad groups are converting visitors into customers. Google has answered this issue very elegantly thanks to the creation of conversion tracking.

Conversion tracking is a way to track when a visitor clicks to a specific page in your website, e.g. when a visitor clicks 'Buy Now' from your sales page and moves to the order summary page (see Fig. 12 for the conversion tracking process. All you have to do is create an action (which can be a sale, a sign-up, or the viewing of a key page) in your AdWords account and Google gives you a line of code which you put on the page your prospects arrive on after they complete your desired action.

FIGURE 12 **CONVERSION TRACKING PROCESS**

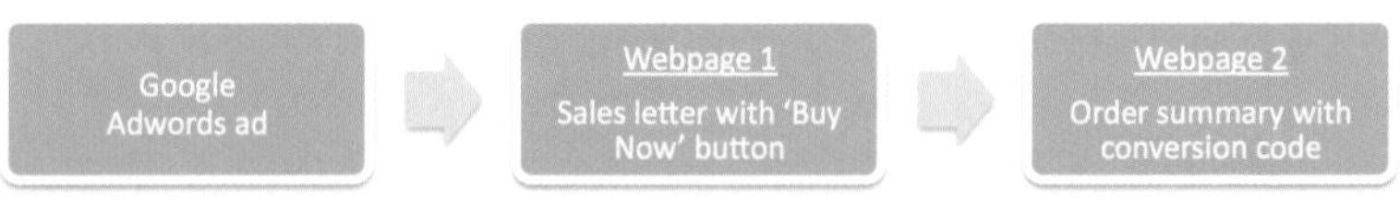

Let's say you want to measure how many people sign up for your free newsletter and determine which ad groups are the most successful. You would therefore place the conversion code on the page prospects are taken to after signing up. This way, you can tell – down to the penny – how much each sign-up is costing you.

You can find Conversion Tracking under the Tools Menu of your AdWords Account (see Fig. 13).

FIGURE 13 **CONVERSION TRACKING LOCATION**

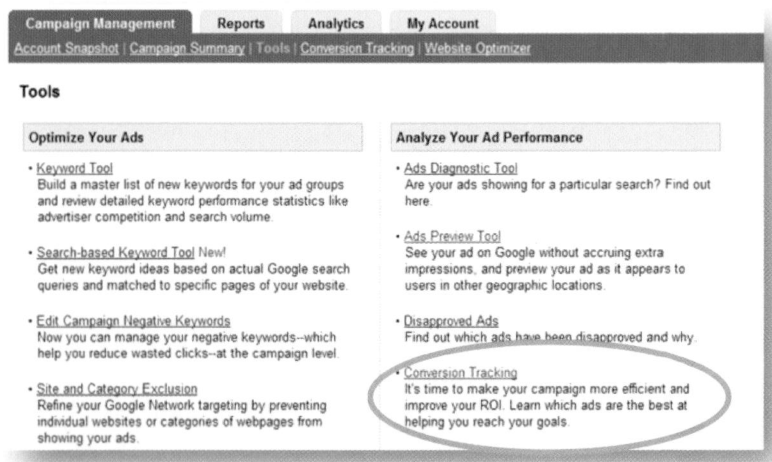

At some point you'll get a notice from Google saying 'Budget Alert! Your ads are only receiving 44% [or whatever number] of their possible impressions.' They'll then show you graphs indicating how you could receive more clicks than you ever dreamed …

Let me set the record straight, because Google sure as hell won't: Google makes money on clicks, you make money on conversions. Before you open the floodgates, check which ad groups are currently costing you the most money. In my experience, ad groups that receive the most clicks aren't the highest converting, though they are likely to receive the lion's share of any new traffic resulting from your increase in budget. This can – though not necessarily – wreak havoc on your return on investment (ROI).

To illustrate this, let's say you have two ad groups, A and B, with a current budget of $10 / £6 per day. Group A receives about $3 / £2 of clicks per day with a cost/conversion of $0.50 / £0.35. Group B receives $7 / £4.50 of clicks with a cost/conversion of $1 / £0.65. Now let's say you take Google's recommendation and increase your budget to $30 / £20 per day. Guess what? Group A still receives about $3 / £2 per day in clicks, and the lackluster Group B is pulling in $27 / £18. Let's look at the numbers, as shown in Tables 5 and 6.

TABLE 5 **AD SPEND vs CONVERSION RATE – BEFORE**

	Ad spend per day	**Cost/ conversion**	**Conversions**
Group A	$3	$0.50	6
Group B	$7	$1.00	7
Total	$10	$0.77	13

TABLE 6 **AD SPEND vs CONVERSION RATE – AFTER**

	Ad spend per day	**Cost/ conversion**	**Conversions**
Group A	$3	$0.50	6
Group B	$27	$1.00	27
Total	$30	$0.91	33

Ouch. Now your cost per conversion has increased to \$0.91 / £0.60. This may not be a deal-breaker if you're making \$2 / £1.30 per click, but if you return-per-click (RPC) is \$0.85 / £0.55, you'll find your business sinking faster than the US auto industry.

This leads me to one last AdWords tip you won't find in the training center. Under the Account Settings, there's a setting that says 'Optimize: Serve the best performing ad.' While this sounds great, the 'best performing' ad is in fact the ad that receives the most clicks – thereby making Google the most money – not the ad that leads to the most conversions. You'll want to change this to the standard setting ASAP.

Google AdWords setup: first 30-day outline

Phase I

- Establish website goals. What does your sales funnel look like? Are you using a sales page, or collecting contact information by offering something for free?
- Analyze current website. How you can you use your website to achieve your goals? Look at your landing pages. It could be one simple sales letter, or several highly targeted to a specific keyword. Guess which I recommend?
- Define and review top online competitors. Where are they dropping the ball? Are they missing a market segment that you could capitalize on? Which keywords are they bidding on? Are there other phrases that may be cheaper?

Phase II

- Review your ads. Create two versions of the most highly trafficked ads. Over time, choose those with the highest conversions.
- Review all keyword campaigns. Which keywords are making you money, and which ones are costing you more than Paul McCartney's ex-wife? Like your ads, review your keywords and fire the losers.

- Review campaign restrictions, filters and negative keyword selection. Increase your geographic targeting, add negative keywords, and filter out websites that aren't providing you with profits.

NEGATIVE KEYWORDS

Negative keywords are terms you don't want your ads appearing for.

The most common negative keyword is 'free.' After all, you don't want to be paying for clicks when someone isn't in a buying frame of mind, so by including 'free' as a negative keyword, you'll prevent your ads showing when someone enters 'free ________.'

Negative keywords also improve your relevancy. For example, if you sell fried chicken recipes, your ads may appear for 'French fried potatoes,' 'Chicken farms,' or 'Beef recipes.' By adding the terms 'potatoes,' 'farms,' and 'beef' as negative keywords (none of which have anything to do with fried chicken recipes), you will sharpen your relevancy, improve your CTR, improve your conversions and lower your advertising cost. Not bad for two minutes work, huh?

AdWords professional exam

If you see yourself creating numerous AdWords campaigns in the near future, it pays to study for the AdWords professional exam (https://adwords.google.com/select/ProfessionalWelcome). When you pass this exam Google awards you with $500 / £330 worth of advertising credits, which can be used on new campaigns ($100 / £65 each for five campaigns). I routinely use these credits to test different products and markets. It's also how I determined the title of this book.

How? Rather than pick a title off the top of my head, I wanted to craft one that was proven to catch people's attention. I created a simple AdWords campaign linking to one of our existing websites and tested six different headlines. The headline with the highest CTR was deemed the winner. This way, my title was guaranteed to turn heads, and it didn't cost me a thing.

In addition to the advertising credits, you also receive numerous marketing materials which can be used when presenting to potential clients (should you decide to freelance as an AdWords specialist down the road).

GOOGLE ADWORDS RESOURCES

For more information on Google AdWords, I highly recommend the Google Training Center and the indispensable book *Google AdWords for Dummies* by Howie Jacobson, PhD.

Google Analytics

Google Analytics helps you measure where your visitors are coming from and how they interact with your site. By measuring the proper metrics you will be able to discover which traffic streams are profitable and which ones are costing you money. There's so much to know about Google Analytics that I could write a book on this topic; however, once you grasp the basic concepts you can begin improving your advertising campaigns right away. Here are the metrics I swear by:

- **Unique page views** – the number of pages viewed by a new visitor (this is a much more important metric than page views). For example, if 10 people visit your site and all 10 of them returned three times, your page views would be 40 while your unique page views would still be 10.

- **Goals** – a desired outcome on your website. For example, this could be reaching a thank you page for newsletter sign-ups, a purchase confirmation page, or any other page on your site that you feel is especially valuable. Bear in mind that at the moment Google only allows you to place four goals on your site.

ADWORDS AND ANALYTICS: TWO SIDES OF THE SAME COIN

For clarification, AdWords is Google's advertising program, and Analytics is their tracking program. If you have both, make sure they are linked together so you can access all your Analytics data from the AdWords interface.

Sometimes the two overlap. In AdWords you can add conversion tracking to your sites which measure the effectiveness of your specific ads. In Analytics, you can do the same thing by setting up a Goal. My advice is to add both to your site and use whichever is appropriate.

At a glance, you will be able to tell how much each ad group costs-per-click (CPC) versus its return-per-click (RPC). When you've let your AdWords campaign run and gathered enough data, it is simply a matter of deleting the unprofitable ad groups and keeping the profitable ones in order to improve your return on investment.

Make sure to remove your own website activity from the reports. To do this, add your IP address as a filter under the Analytics settings page. If you don't know your IP address, go to www.whatismyipaddress.com to find out. When you're ready, go to www.stream-life.com to watch an example of how I set up an Analytics account.

In order to use Analytics, you must first sign up for a free account at www.google.com/analytics. The most important thing to do is add the Google Analytics code to all your web pages. Over time, you'll have many questions about your campaigns such as:

- 'Which keywords convert best for sign-ups and purchases? Do some only convert for sign-ups?'
- 'In which positions are my ads on the content network? If they're first, am I paying too much for each click?'
- 'Which landing pages are costing me money? Which ones are making money hand over fist?'

Google Analytics is a great tool, and should be one of the first things you add to your site. It measures not only your AdWords traffic, but also traffic you receive from the search engines. In order to increase traffic from the search, you need to improve your search engine optimization.

Search engine optimization (SEO)

Search engine optimization, also known as SEO, is a way of getting your website to the top of the search engines so people can find your company more easily and faster. Think about this for a moment ... If your website is the first listing to display after entering a keyword, you could be receiving hundreds – even thousands – of visitors for free! SEO can save you money on advertising and should be a primary weapon in your marketing arsenal.

Recognize the top search engines

In order for your website to get to the top of the search engines, you'll need to know the top ranking search engines:

- Google.com
- Yahoo.com
- MSN.com
- YouTube.com

Conduct SEO research

Use the strategies described in the section on market research to discover keywords that are routinely searched for online. To recap, you will need to:

- **Use relevant SEO keywords.** To see what your visitors are actually searching for, use WordTracker or the Google AdWords tool, enter a keyword you think people are searching for in the search box, and click enter. Make a note of the keywords with more than 10 searches per day – anything less isn't a fishing hole, it's a puddle.

- **Analyze the competition.** Visit a search engine and search for your keywords in quotes. Determine:
  - How many competitors there are? (Less than 5,000 in quotes is good.)
  - How many words are in bold? (Do your competitors use the keywords on their web pages?)
  - What's the quality like of your competitors' websites ('Bob's Blog' or the New York Times)?
- **Find an underserved niche market.** If you have competitive keywords, try to create a niche market by focusing on regions and specialized terms.

How search engines work

Before we get into SEO practices, you need to have a basic understanding of how search engines work.

1. **Get crawled.** Search engines send out programs known as spiders to 'crawl' or scan your web pages to determine if the information is valuable (original content and linked to by other websites). If it is valuable, the web page will be added to the search engine index – all the web pages that display in the search engines.
2. **Get indexed.** If your pages were crawled and added to the search engine index, the information will show up in the search results. Only web pages that are indexed will show up in the search results. Notice I said web pages, not websites. Most websites – especially large ones – will not have every page indexed. There are simply too many pages of information for the search engines to effectively store them all, so they have to be picky.

In a nutshell, your goals are the following:

- Invite spiders to crawl your website.
- Convince them to index your web pages.
- Show up on the first page of the search engine for your keyword.

Sounds easy, huh? Well, the first two are. You can have that done within a matter of hours by submitting a site map (which we'll get to in a second). Moving up in the search rankings, however, is a long-term – dare I say ongoing – battle. How do websites move to the top of the search results? They make it simple for search engines to read their site (known as 'on-page optimization') while increasing the quantity and quality of websites that link to them (known as 'off-page optimization').

Let's look at how you optimize your website both on and off the page.

SEO: on-page

In order to get your site listed higher in the search engines without paying a thing, use effective web design.

Tags

On every web page there is a place for you to add meta tags – a web page element that displays information about the page, such as title, keywords, and description. This information is not seen on the web page itself, but is in the source code; this helps the search engines understand the key points behind your web page. You can view the meta tags for any web page by right-clicking on the web page and selecting 'View Source' or 'View Page Source.' Toward the top of the source you'll see several tags for title, keywords and description.

When creating your web pages be sure to add tags for the following:

- **Title tags** – indicate the title and subject of a web page while blending keywords in the text.
- **Description tags** – indicate the description of a web page. Your description may appear in the search engine's results, so make sure it conveys your value as quickly as possible and blend keywords into the description.
- **Keyword tags** – indicate the main keywords for the web page. They should be separated by a comma, not a space. For example, if you are optimizing for 'fried chicken recipes,' 'fried chicken gravy,' and 'fried

chicken meals,' you would enter them as follows: Fried chicken recipes, fried chicken gravy, fried chicken meals. Don't add more than five to ten keywords in the tag – I generally use between one and five, and prefer to get on with more important tasks.

Keywords

You will use keywords not only in your keyword tags, but throughout your web page.

- **Headers and subheaders** (also known as H1 and H2 tags). In web design, there are six headers labeled H1–H6. The higher the number, the less important it seems to the search engines. Think about it: a page with 'Fried Chicken Recipes' as the main headline, and mentioned in several subheads is probably likely to be about … you guessed it, fried chicken recipes. The search engines think the same way. Ensure you use only H1 and H2 for your keywords.
- **Image descriptions.** Make sure you enter keywords as your image descriptions on your website. This is an additional way to place more keywords on your website and add image descriptions.
- **Use keywords text as links.** Instead of saying 'click here' use a keyword such as 'fried chicken recipes.' This is known as 'anchor text' and is one of the most important parts of SEO. Wikipedia is one of the most optimized websites in the world, and is a great resource to emulate. Every page is full of rich, original content with dozens of keyword-optimized anchor texts linking to other pages, which in turn link to other pages, and so on.
- **Name your web pages with keywords.** Give your web pages descriptive names with keywords. For example, instead of naming a web page 'guidebook.html,' try 'fried-chicken-recipes-guidebook.html.' Use dashes '–' to add space between the keywords.
- **Increase keyword density.** The more frequently your keywords are used on your web page, the better. Try to keep your keyword density under 3% as any more than this can be seen as abuse. To find out what your keyword density percentage is, visit

http://tools.seobook.com/general/keyword-density/. As Google states repeatedly, create websites for users, not search engines.

- **Design your keywords.** Not only do you want a lot of keywords in your text, you want to style them bold, italics, and underscored. Do this throughout the text.
- **Keyword placement.** Put the majority of your keywords at the top and bottom of your web pages as this is where search engines place the most emphasis.
- **Stem your keywords.** Instead of repeating the same keywords over and over, use a variation of those keywords. For example, for the keyword 'search' you would also want to incorporate searches, searching, searched, etc.

Navigation

- **Every page links to the home page.** Create a navigation bar on all web pages so the user can get to the home page. If you have a large website with multiple web pages, consider using a HTML template to make this process easier. Remember to use applicable keyword anchor text for each link.
- **Internal links.** You can improve your website's SEO rankings by linking web pages within your website. Remember, it's important to use the applicable keyword as your anchor text.
- **Concise navigation.** When designing your website, never bury web pages more than two folders deep. Users should not have to click more than twice to find what they need or get back to the home page (see Fig. 14).

FIGURE 14 **EXAMPLE SITE MAP**

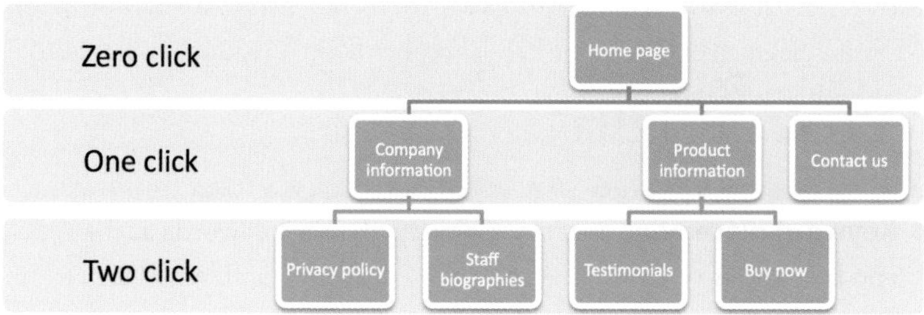

Site map

In order for Google to 'crawl' or scan your website, you need to create a site map and upload it to Google.

- To create a site map, visit www.xml-sitemaps.com.
- To upload your site map to Google, visit www.google.com/webmasters/sitemaps/docs/en/sitemap-generator.html.

Google Webmaster Central (www.google.com/webmasters/) is the best free resource to help you understand how and why your website is showing up in search results. Using this tool, you can determine how many other websites are linking to yours, what keywords your website shows up for, and any problems Google is having crawling and indexing your site.

The Webmaster tool is not updated as often as people would like, which means you may not see results right away. This doesn't mean that websites aren't linking to you; it just isn't showing up in their reports yet. Be patient!

Another common concern is when a website suddenly has far fewer pages indexed than before. If your pages contain original content and are listed in your site map, they won't be de-indexed. So why do the number of pages fluctuate? People tend to think of Google as one computer in one location, when it's actually thousands of servers in locations around the world. Information takes a while to update across the system, so you may be getting reports from a server in California on Monday, then a completely different report from Virginia on Tuesday. Remember, patience is a virtue.

You'll find examples of on-page optimization at www.stream-life.com.

SEO: off-page

Now that we've covered what you can do on your own website to improve your SEO, it's time find other websites that will link to you. Linking has really become the name of the game in SEO these days and rightfully so. In the past, search engines would look more at a web page's content, whereas now they take into account how many other people find that web page (or website) useful. The more websites that link to yours, the more valuable you appear to users and the more likely you'll rank highly for your keywords.

Of course, a thousand links from small websites aren't nearly as valuable as one link from a highly trusted authority site. This is true in the offline world as well: an economics professor from Harvard who has been interviewed on CNN will carry more weight than a junior college professor who's conducted a thousand interviews with college radio stations.

When a search engine examines your site, it takes into account the quantity and quality of other websites that are linking to yours. Think of each link as a vote for your website – the more votes from trusted sites, the better.

Baby got backlinks

So how does one find these high-authority sites and convince them to link to your website? There are several methods at your disposal:

- **Google Alerts** (www.google.com/alerts) will automatically update you on sites related to your niche, as well as any breaking news.

- **Trusted publications** can provide you with a list of highly respected sites in your field. For example, if you run a travel site, search for '25 Best Travel Sites.' Contact as many of these as you can and request a link. Of course, you should give them a damned good reason why they should. I look at each website and see if they accept proposals for writing projects. If they do, and provide links to the author's website, I'll contact them with a proposal. This method is a win–win–win: the authority site receives a quality article, our website receives a valuable backlink, and we receive traffic from people who have read the article and are interested to learn more.

- **Directory submissions.** List your website with as many high PageRank directories as possible. Google has mentioned this is no longer as important as it once was, so don't knock yourself out submitting to hundreds. Pick 50 to 100 and crank it out one afternoon. Two stand out among the rest and deserve special mention: Dmoz.org (which is free, but damned hard to get into) and Yahoo Directory ($300 / £200 – but pretty easy to get into after that).

- **Article directories.** While covered in detail in the section on article marketing, it should be mentioned here as well. Write an article your market would be interested in, and submit it to the article directories with a backlink to your site at the end of the article. When other websites republish your article your backlink will appear on their site as well.

- **Bait people.** Create pages that are of such incredibly high value people can't help but link to them. This is known as 'link-bait' and is a very popular method of promotion among bloggers. Choose a topic most people struggle with and write about it to death. Provide a comprehensive guide to a hot topic (e.g. Firefox extensions, fried chicken cooking methods, airport taxes, whatever), and authority sites will eventually see it and link to you.

BACKLINK BUILDER

Wanna save a bundle of time on SEO? Get Backlink Builder (http://www.easybacklinkbuilder.com/). This service supplies you with 30 high PR websites you can link to. For a measly $5 / £3.50 a month, you can find yourself on the first page of Google in no time. I use this service for all my sites.

SEO on-page and off-page checklist

Use the checklist in Table 7 to ensure your website is properly optimized for SEO.

SEO tools

- **WordTracker** (www.WordTracker.com)
- **Google Ad Preview Tool** (https://AdWords.google.com/select/AdTargetingPreviewTool)
- **Keyword Density** (http://tools.seobook.com/general/keyword-density/
- **Google's Guide to SEO** (www.google.com/webmasters/docs/search-engine-optimization-starter-guide.pdf)
- **Create Site maps** (www.xml-sitemaps.com)
- **Google Site maps** (www.google.com/webmasters/sitemaps/docs/en/sitemap-generator.html)
- **Google Webmaster Central** (www.google.com/webmasters/)
- **Google Alerts** (www.google.com/alerts)

TABLE 7 **SEO ON-PAGE AND OFF-PAGE CHECKLIST**

Topics	**Details**
URL	Include keywords in your web page file names (e.g. (www.YourWebSite.com/keyword.html). The total URL shouldn't be more than 100 characters.
Site map	Create one site map and update it whenever you add new content. Use a site map generator and submit it to Google, Yahoo! and MSN
Navigation	Design for ease of use. Keep it clean and professional. Make sure all web pages are linked.
Site structure	No web page should be more than two clicks away from the home page.
Age	The longer the website has existed, the better your SEO results will be.
Size of site	Large, content-driven sites with dynamic data work best. Update frequently!
Title tags	Write the title of the web page, making sure to include your domain name and keywords, e.g. 'YourWebsiteName: Your Keyword.' No longer than 60 characters.
Keywords tags	Write all web page keywords separated by commas, e.g. 'keyword 1, keyword 2, keyword 3.' No more than five keywords per web page.
Description tags	Write a description of the web page, making sure to include your domain name and keywords. No longer than 200 characters, including spaces.
H1 and H2 tags	Add keywords to header tags.
Formatting	Bold, underscore or italicize keywords.
Keyword density	Not more than 3%.
Keyword stemming	Vary your keywords, e.g. 'run, running and ran.'
Images	Add keyword in <alt tag>.
Internal links	Use anchor text.
Outbound links	Only link to quality sites and use anchor text!
Backlinks	Don't buy links, or work with sites that are nothing but links (known as link farms). Use Backlink Builder to add your website to one new high PageRank website every day. Use anchor text.

Blog with WordPress.org

If you intend to focus all your long-term efforts on one website, it may behoove you to create a blog. By continually adding fresh content that people will find valuable, not only will your relationships improve with your existing customer base, you'll also increase the number of backlinks helping your SEO. I've run blogs in the past, but due to the large number of niches that I work in, they are no longer cost-effective to maintain.

If you are interested in learning more about blogging, from design tips to real-life examples of producing quality content, I strongly advise you to check out www.skelliewag.org. This is one of the best blogs out there, and along with its sister site www.anywired.com you can learn a lot about blogging and working online. Anywired remains the only blog I've ever subscribed to.

There is ongoing debate about the best platform for blogs. WordPress.org (www.wordpress.org) is the most robust platform, with thousands of different themes to help customize your blog. As an added benefit, this blog platform allows you to create SEO friendly blog posts simply with the click of a button.

Now that you have some key ideas for SEO, let's take a look at an incredibly powerful form of traffic generation known as article marketing.

Article marketing

One of the most popular forms of search engine optimization, article marketing is the submission of original pieces of writing to article directories for syndication, allowing other websites to republish your article on their own site with a link to yours. It's a win–win: the other sites publish useful content on their site, and you receive additional links and traffic to your own site.

Below is what you need to do in order to fully take advantage of article marketing.

Research the demand

Go to WordTracker and type in a general phrase you'd like to optimize for. For example, if your site is about dogs, you would type in 'dogs.' WordTracker gives you a list of the top searches associated with this term, such as 'dog training,' 'dog food,' and 'how to stop your dog from barking.' To the right of these terms you will see the estimated daily search volume; this gives you an idea of how many people are looking for this phrase. For our purposes, you need to have at least five to ten daily searches.

WORDTRACKER: the definitive keyword research tool

There is no doubt that WordTracker (www.WordTracker.com) is as indispensible as it is expensive. At the time of writing, they charged nearly $70 / £45 per month, which is too high for most newcomers to the market. This is no accident; the folks at WordTracker know they've got the best game in town, and professionals in SEO don't bat an eye at forking out the $300 / £200 annual fee to give them the added advantage. When you figure that proper keyword research results in free traffic, $300 / £200 is a small price to pay for a year's worth of advertising.

So what are your other options?

Try the Google keyword tool (https://AdWords.google.com/select/KeywordToolExternal), or the free (albeit highly limited) version of WordTracker. Currently, WordTracker offers a free seven-day trial that includes a crash course in SEO. Research as many keywords/niches as possible during that time and get to work!

Research the competition

Now that you know how many searches a given keyword receives every day, you need to find out how many other sites are optimized for that same keyword. To do this, use the AdWords Preview Tool and type the keyword in quotation marks. The quotation marks show websites that have that exact phrase at least once.

What you're looking for are phrases in quotation marks the return fewer than 5,000 results; research has shown this is not a very competitive keyword, and you can quickly find yourself on the first page of Google.

How? There are a few sites that Google is absolutely head-over-heels in love with. Ever notice how often Wikipedia shows up for searches on people and places? Or how about YouTube for 'how to' searches? The key is to get your work that is optimized for a keyword on one of these trusted, high-ranking sites.

Remember, search engines show results for pages that are;

- highly optimized for the keyword;
- from a highly trusted site.

Therefore, even though your website is mired in obscurity, you can still get your highly optimized content noticed by sharing it with highly trusted sites.

One of Google's most loved websites is EzineArticles. You can very easily find an article you submit to them in the top 10 results on Google within a matter of days. Granted, this isn't your site, but it's a great way to gain exposure for keywords too competitive to rank for initially (because an article from EZA is more likely to rank highly for a term).

So is article marketing the wave of the future? Should you create a one-page website and write hundreds of articles sending traffic to it? I'm afraid this is the approach held by many online marketers and is short-sighted. Your priority should always be to build the value of your own website, and while links from articles will help, you eventually want your own web pages to show up for those keywords. At best, only 10% of people who read your articles will click through to your site. Wouldn't you rather reap 100% of the traffic?

Research the advertisers

When looking at the number of search results for a given keyword, record the number of sponsored links on a page. This is important to note because the higher the number of paid advertisers for that keyword, the more profitable it may be.

In summary, you want the following:

- a high number of daily searches (at least five to ten);
- a low number of optimized competition (no more than 5,000);
- a high number of paid advertisers (the more the better).

As I mentioned earlier, this is a strategy that costs nothing but takes more time. If you are serious about keyword research, WordTracker is the only way to go.

Once you've selected ten keywords that fit these criteria, it's time to start writing articles. Sign up for an account at www.EzineArticles.com. This will allow you to write and submit ten articles initially; once they've been accepted you have unlimited submissions. Make sure you read the author's guidelines before submitting them (they get approved much faster).

There are two reasons for writing articles:

1. Traffic from the articles themselves.
2. Backlinks to your site, which will improve your results in the search engines.

Only rookies and the near-sighted use article marketing just for the traffic. The key is to build up your website's reputation – the initial traffic is just the cherry on top.

If you want your article to show up high in search engine results, you need to optimize the article itself for your specific keyword. Be sure to include the keyword in your article title (preferably at the beginning), your first paragraph, and your conclusion.

If you want your website to show up high in the search engine results, you won't have to optimize your article as much. In a perfect world, your website would be number one on Google and your articles filling positions two to ten. However, due to the high PageRank of article directories it's very common to see them score higher on the results page, even if they are linking to your website!

Still, it's better to compete against yourself, which is why I recommend optimizing your articles and using similar anchor text to your website. After all, someone else could write a similar, more optimized article and steal your traffic.

At the end of each article, there is a resource box where you include a bio and links to your site. This is the most important part of the article: a well structured resource box will drive highly targeted traffic to your site. In addition, you should use appropriate anchor text. Below are examples of how you should – and shouldn't – structure your bio box.

The wrong way

> *John Smith is a world renowned business expert, whose core competencies include business analysis, value investing, and foreign investment market analysis. To learn more about John and his company, click here to access his website.*

Huh? Even if John's article is dynamite, very few people click through to his website for a number of reasons. First of all, there is no specific value offered to them for visiting his site. Second, there isn't a call to action. Third, we learned nothing about John or his business from this bio, nor is it a very catchy opening to grab the reader's attention. People's eyes will glaze over when they reach this bio, and John's business will suffer.

The right way

> *Stop wasting money! Your investments could be a ticking time bomb, waiting to blow up in light of a foreign exchange crash. Visit our website and receive your very own free, customized report from a trained foreign investment advisor. Act now!*

As you can see, this bio catches the reader's attention from the first sentence by highlighting a major pain point. It demonstrates value to the reader with the free customized report (in exchange for their contact information) and makes use of applicable anchor text for search engine optimization.

With that in mind, it makes sense to create as many articles as possible and submit those articles to several article directories.

Of course, quality trumps quantity. Ignore any services that offer to submit your article to dozens of directories. I've only seen results from a handful.

Article marketing tools

Here are the article directories I submit to:

- www.EzineArticles.com
- www.Goarticles.com
- www.Articledashboard.com
- www.ArticleAlley.com

The best thing about article marketing is that you can get started now. Choose a keyword, write an article, and link to your site using keywords as your anchor text. Once your article is approved, you'll see traffic almost instantly. Total time invested: 30–40 minutes.

Article marketing teaches you how to create content that is precise and concise. These articles can be used to increase your results in the search engines while providing a steady stream of traffic. If used properly, your articles can make money selling other people's products through affiliate networks.

Affiliate marketing

Affiliate marketing involves a product developer paying commissions on sales to another party for marketing his product. Let's take a look at the two roles in affiliate marketing:

- The merchant creates a product/service and pays a commission.
- The affiliate markets the merchant's product/service to make a commission.

I play both of these roles and will market other people's products to my newsletter subscribers while allowing others to promote my products for a generous commission (usually 70% per sale). Using affiliates is a great strategy for increasing your exposure: PPC and SEO are incredibly powerful but somewhat limited in scope.

How? Let's say someone is interested in marketing your product. Rather than optimize around keywords or create PPC campaigns – both of which you currently do – they fire off an e-mail to their newsletter subscribers describing your product in a positive light. Assuming they provide real value in their correspondence, their subscribers are more inclined to purchase the product.

You cannot find customers with this element of trust through SEO or PPC. Rather than arrive at your site cautious, confused, and skeptical, they are recommended from a third party they have grown to trust and are in effect pre-sold on you and what you can offer them.

The affiliate: marketing other people's products

All you need to do is sign up with an affiliate directory like ClickBank or Commission Junction. They will give you a specific line of code to add to your links (so they can keep track of who sold what). Make sure to include this specific reference when you link to an affiliate's sales page. Becoming an affiliate is free; you only pay if you decide to list your own product for other people to sell.

There are several successful ways to market other people's products.

Create a review site and link to affiliates

This can be very lucrative, but you must have first-hand knowledge of the product in question. If you don't you are attempting to profit at someone else's expense. We follow a simple rule: never include an affiliate link if we don't personally use and receive value from the product.

By following this rule, everyone wins:

- The creator of the product gets more sales.
- The buyer purchases a product that provides real value.
- Visitors to our site can access the information for free, thanks to the revenue these links provide.
- Only then do I (the affiliate) deserve to get paid.

Let that sink in: as an affiliate, you are only entitled to profit if you bring real value to your visitors.

Recommend a product to your newsletter

After working in this industry for a while, I've come to suspect that many so-called 'free' newsletters are little more than sales pitches for affiliate products. While they may or may not make money, they provide little value to their visitors and must constantly strive to get more traffic.

Having said that, I have actually gone out of my way to click on someone's link because of the value they have brought to me. For example, Dr Howie Jacobson, author of Google AdWords for Dummies, has provided key insights to my business model over the past year and a half. When he sent out a recommendation for a new product, I wasn't that interested at the time. But I kept the e-mail (which he had pointed out contained an affiliate link, always a good strategy). Several months later the product rose in priority, and I went back to that e-mail and purchased the product, just so he could get his referral fee. This is achieved by providing someone with real value and stating publicly that you will profit from the relationship.

The merchant: finding affiliates to sell your products

If you currently sell a product, you can list your ad in an affiliate marketplace such as ClickBank. Be sure to include information about your product, a copy of the sales page, and what percentage of each sale you give to affiliates.

Sharp business people go above and beyond and will provide template e-mails for newsletters, promotional discounts, and PPC ads with their historical results (should you want to advertise this way). Believe it or not, there are people out there who use Google AdWords to promote other people's products as their sole business model, and they make a ton of cash doing it.

However, my advice is to create your own products so you ensure total control over your business model. You don't want the merchant to change their price, provide less-than-satisfactory customer service, or pull the product and kill your business. Create your own product and begin building a list, then occasionally recommend one of these products to your audience.

I also recommend offering the largest commission possible to your affiliates. They shoulder the majority of risk marketing a merchant's product and should be compensated accordingly. In short, you'll earn more if you offer more.

Options for creating an affiliate program

As a merchant, there are two routes you can go with affiliate programs:

- Join an existing affiliate network.
- Create your own from the ground up.

Joining an affiliate program is quick and easy … in theory. I have had products denied by www.ClickBank.net, with no explanation given.

You should also try http://www.e-junkie.com which has an affiliate program that you manage yourself, and like the rest of their services, it rocks! I recommend this for anyone wanting to get started right away with affiliates.

Once your streams start to take off, you may want to develop your own affiliate program. You can buy PostAffiliatePro for $150 / £100 – plus an optional $300 / £200 for installation – and start right away. While you have complete control over the relationship, there isn't a built-in marketplace for you to list your product, which makes you solely responsible for recruiting affiliates. If you're up to it, research the top sites in your market and approach the owners with a personalized e-mail (or, God forbid, call them), demonstrating your knowledge of their site and how marketing your product can be mutually beneficial.

Most affiliates are looking for quality products that convert well, have a low refund rate and offer generous (+$50 / £35) commissions. By offering additional marketing materials, you set yourself above other merchants. You have a choice: set up the marketing materials for affiliates once, or expect each one to start from scratch. Remember Archimedes: leverage your efforts by doing the work once and help your affiliates – and you – make more money. Set up autoresponders and send them new marketing ideas, ask them for feedback, create pre-sell pages for them, five-day autoresponder templates, product reviews, etc. An affiliate should take less than an hour to set up an income stream with your stream.

Video marketing: the quantum leap

Video marketing is marketing your website, product or service through video. Its popularity will grow and it will change the way search engines work in the future. At the time of writing, YouTube is now the second-largest search engine in the world (behind Google). If you aren't using video to market your products, you're leaving money on the table.

YouTube: the best thing since Google

There is no doubt in my mind that YouTube will be the definitive source for video marketing in the future. Like search engine optimization, it is imperative to understand the algorithm behind YouTube before you begin your marketing efforts.

YouTube is owned by Google, and it should be no surprise that this website follows a similar algorithm. Unlike Google, it is possible to make it to the home page of YouTube, which can result in thousands of new visitors visiting your website within a matter of hours. In order to rank well, you must understand how the game of video marketing plays out. It all boils down to 'honors.'

YouTube distributes honors according to the number of comments, favorites, ratings, and views. Naturally, if you are able to dominate any of these aspects, you will improve your rankings and see your traffic soar.

Here are several tips that will help you develop your video marketing strategy when it comes to your streams:

1. **Keep it fresh.** Just like many other search engines, YouTube adores websites that are able to provide updated content on a regular basis. This is because the algorithm rewards freshness.
2. **Maintain a high profile.** You can crush the competition using video marketing by strengthening your profile. Like many forums, your profile will eventually come into play. In order to substantially improve your profile, create videos that are viral in nature – the

more views your videos have, the stronger your profile. Submitting a video from a new account without subscribers or friends will hinder your ability to rank high for a given key phrase.

3. **Relevance is key.** Your success depends mainly upon the type of channels that you choose. If you create videos targeted toward a small niche and receive a relatively high number of views you will receive honors quickly.

4. **Get your share on.** For every video you create there is a share option. Obviously, the more friends you happen to have, the larger your sphere of influence becomes. In addition, this type of leverage can come in handy when promoting your site using social media such as Digg or Stumble Upon.

5. **The beauty of bulletins.** This is a simple way to reach all of your friends. Post a message on the bulletin board and everyone will be able to access your new video via your profile page.

6. **Subscribers, subscribers, subscribers.** Much like blogging, you can invite viewers to subscribe to your feed. This guarantees that they will remain in your sales funnel for months if not years to come.

7. **Network.** Ah, the power of social media. With the click of a button you can now submit your video to Stumble Upon, Digg, Facebook, and MySpace.

8. **Never under- (or over-) estimate the power of friends and family.** This is your ace in the hole – when you've created a video guaranteed to spread virally, send it to everyone you know personally. However, this method may backfire on you if misdirected – send your video only if it's applicable to your loved ones, or risk being blacklisted from family gatherings!

9. **Relevance is key.** As with the other major search engines, success is predicated upon relevance. Don't stretch your marketing efforts so far as to miss the mark. Keep it simple, keep it direct.

10. **Keep it brief.** Your video should not exceed two minutes, period. Attention spans are short on the Internet, especially when it comes to video. You can lose prospects – and customers – if your video doesn't quickly capture their interest.

11. **Keep it moving.** A static image should not remain on your screen for more than three to five seconds. You are dealing with a very short attention span, so keep viewers stimulated.

12. **Watch more TV.** People are programmed to the rhythms found in television advertising. Create your video with a similar tempo and you'll hold their attention longer.

13. **Convey a strong message with a strong voice.** OK, we don't all sound like Barry White. If you can get someone you know who has acting or radio experience to record your message, it will certainly improve the end product.

14. **Use a solid soundtrack.** Music can make all the difference. It fills the dead space between your words and engages the viewer on another level. For example, if your video is intended to provide stress relief, you can play relaxing classical music (like a Lexus commercial).

15. **Repetition is key.** Repetition is key. Repetition is ... Create catch phrases to drive your point home, and repeat them throughout the video. This happens all the time in television: 'The Best a Man Can Get,' 'We're Lovin' It,' and of course, 'Got Milk?' Pick a slogan and drill it into your prospects' heads.

16. **Integrate text and graphics with your narration.** One of video's main advantages over text is the incorporation of sound and imagery within your message. While your narrator speaks, be sure to tie in applicable key points and pictures.

17. **Provide a solid intro.** How many times have you skipped a video that provides a long-winded intro? For example, if you are searching for a video on how to make pad thai, you'll get sick and tired of watching videos that start with 'Hi, I'm so-and-so from

who-cares.com, and today we are going to make pad thai. This is a common noodle dish in Thailand, and …' After the second or third video, you get frustrated. I do this all the time, which is why I make damn sure my videos are engaging and highly relevant to the viewer from the first frame.

18. **Respond to other videos.** Use videos as a response to other videos on YouTube in order to maximize your exposure.

By incorporating video into your marketing arsenal, you will gain not only new visitors to your websites, you'll be staking your claim early in what proves to be one of the fastest-growing sectors of online search. Visit www.youtube.com to get started.

Traffic jam: which method should I use?

Let's recap the main methods of driving traffic to your website:

- **Pay-per-click (PPC).** This method provides the most control and immediate results, but at a price. Test your products validity, and split test your ads/offers until you find the winners. Start with Google, then open accounts with Yahoo! and MSN once you are confident with your results. Why start with Google? You'll get the largest amount of traffic, and it provides advertisers with more control over their campaigns.
- **Affiliate marketing.** Once your sales letter is proven to convert, start offering commissions to affiliates. If your product is digital you can offer larger commissions than tangible goods. I personally offer my affiliates anywhere between 50 and 75% of the retail value. Other marketers offer as much as 100% in the hope they'll make money on follow-up offers.
- **Search engine optimization (SEO).** Do your research and determine where your competitive advantages are. Which keywords are being searched for with low competition? Target these phrases, incorporate them into your landing pages, and start building links using those terms in your anchor text.

- **Article marketing.** From your SEO research, choose keywords that are too competitive for your website, and instead write a keyword optimized article and submit it to high-PageRank directories like EzineArticles. Use the keywords for which your web pages are optimized in your anchor text.

Depending on the stream you chose, your marketing efforts will need to be customized. Focus your energy on the marketing tactics shown in Table 8 in the suggested numerical order.

TABLE 8 **METHODS OF DRIVING TRAFFIC TO STREAMS**

	Product development stream	Content-driven stream	Affiliate network stream
Pay-per-click	1		1
Affiliate marketing (as a merchant)	2		
Search engine optimization	3	1	2
Article marketing	4	2	3 optional

I don't include video marketing in this section because it works well for any media and can be used at any time. In order to support your SEO campaign, you can title your videos with specific keywords and use anchor text to link back to your site.

If you decide to create a blog for your business, incorporate it into your SEO strategy. While you should optimize your posts for specific keywords, a blog will grow much faster by appealing to humans, not search engines.

PPC AND SEO CONSULTANTS

Once you get your feet wet and want to bring in some pros to fine-tune your campaigns, check out these guys:

Getting started: Earning under $2,000 / £1,320 per month

- SEMPO (www.sempo.org): see the member directory (tel. 1-781-876-8866)
- Warrior Forum (www.warriorforum.com): ask around for PPC and SEO help – this place is crawling with consultants

Mid-range: Earning between $2,000 / £1,320 and $5,000 / £3,300 per month

- Clicks 2 Customers (www.clicks2customers.com)
- Working Planet (www.workingplanet.com; tel. 1-401-709-3123)

High end: Don't call until you're bringing in at least $5,000 / £3,300 to $10,000 / £6,600 per month

- Did It (www.did-it.com; tel. 1-800-932-7761)
- David Viney (http://www.seo-expert-services.co.uk/; tel. 44 (0) 845-050-9414)
- iProspect (www.iprospect.com; tel. 1-617-923-7000)
- Marketing Experiments (www.marketingexperiments.com)

Once your website starts receiving considerable traffic, you will need to further refine your efforts through split testing in order to maximize your return on investment (ROI).

Testing and refinement

Testing, testing, testing ... this is the equivalent of 'location, location, location' in real estate. There comes a time in all Internet marketers' lives when they realize that testing is a vital practice to improve their business.

Let's begin with a primer on the various methods of testing.

A/B split testing

A/B split testing is delivering two different marketing messages in the hopes of improving conversion rates. Back in the days before the Internet, direct marketers would send out mass mailings, half of which would contain one message, the other half a different message. When the sales or phone calls started rolling in, the results were tallied and a winner was declared. This is a long and costly process. Now you can split test many aspects of your online business in a matter of seconds.

Pay-per-click ads

Anyone using PPC should definitely run split tests on their ads. It takes perhaps ten seconds to write a new ad (known as the 'treatment') and test it against the original (known as the 'control'). I've seen conversion rates jump from 16 to 20.4% over the course of four split tests.

Pay-per-click ads are easy to set up and give you the ability to test two radically different approaches (Fig. 15). After running an A/B split test, you might notice that one ad converts significantly better or worse than the other. You keep the winner as the control and create another treatment to challenge it. Over time you have created several winners and dramatically increased your conversions.

FIGURE 15 **EXAMPLE OF GOOGLE ADWORDS ADS**

When conducting an A/B split test you should only test one component at a time to ensure accuracy. If you were to split test two radically different web pages, it would be impossible to tell exactly which factors helped declare a winner. Was it the headline? A different logo? Sales copy? Background color? You'll never know for certain, and that uncertainty can lead to unfounded conclusions. The answer to this uncertainty can be found using what's known as multi-variable testing.

Multi-variable testing: Taguchi testing

This can help you determine which factor contributed to success/failure. With multivariable testing you can test several aspects at a time and know for certain which factors contributed to success, which contributed to failure, and which were non-performers.

Taguchi testing

This is a brief and possibly unnecessary history of Taguchi testing. The Taguchi method was created in the 1950s in order to reduce manufacturing costs for carmakers; up until then it was very expensive for them to test new ideas. After employing the Taguchi method, Japanese carmakers found themselves leading the industry while American manufacturers such as Ford and GM lagged behind. The results of the Taguchi method were so incredible that Ford, out of desperation, decided to give it a shot. It proved to be a good decision: within a short period of time, Ford had created the Taurus, which became the most popular car in America.

So how does the Taguchi method work? As a simple example, say you wanted to test five versions of the headline, logo, and background color of a sales page. In order to thoroughly test all of these options, you would have to create 125 different pages (5 × 5 × 5). Many new websites are lucky to get that number of visits a day, making testing a very lengthy and expensive process.

Taguchi uses orthogonal arrays to cut through this process. Rather than test each and every combination (known as a full factorial experiment) Taguchi systematically tests a smaller sample size selected from the whole (known as fractional factorial experiments) and is able to reach conclusions up to ten times faster.

Needless to say, this is a huge benefit with regard to testing your website. You can now reach the same conclusions in one month with Taguchi testing that would have taken ten months using standard split testing.

And it gets better. As we saw earlier, many split tests will often have a negative impact on your conversion rate – in essence a step backward. Not so with Taguchi.

You see, when you're testing so many different variables simultaneously, you're bound to have a few variables that greatly improve your conversion rate, and these winners will be quickly added to your sales pitch.

However, there are some drawbacks. First and foremost, setting up one of these tests can take an awfully long time as you have to create two to six variations for each variable. Also, there's a steep learning curve when it comes to testing multiple variables; most people new to this method are lucky to find a 5 to 10% increase in their conversion rates. When you factor in the amount of time taken to set up a Taguchi test, it's easy to see why so many people opt for an easier test.

Elements to test

The possibilities of testing are endless, though the following elements tend to play a greater role in improving conversions:

- **Price.** Price your product too high, and your sales go down; price it too low, and you're leaving money on the table. Take your competitors' price and test three price points: what they're offering, 20% less and 20% more. This should give you a good idea as to how price sensitive your market is.

- **Headline.** This is the first thing your prospect sees on the page, so make it count! Try headlines with different angles: ask a question, highlight a main benefit, highlight a pain point, make a bold claim, or say something seemingly nonsensical.
- **Subhead.** Test these together with your headline, or test each one separately.
- **Product image placement.** Should you place your product at the top of your page, or further down? Instead of your product, maybe a logo?
- **Video.** Does video work? Try showing a demo of your product or video testimonials.
- **Guarantee.** Test a standard 'Money Back Guarantee' against a stronger one, where prospects keep the product even if they ask for a refund.
- **PS.** I've seen significant improvement on a sales page just by testing the closing sentence. Like headlines, test different angles for maximum results.
- **Background color/image.** Sales letters on web pages usually have two parts: the letter itself and the background. Test different background colors (I usually try black, blue, and red). Remember that the letter itself should always have dark text on a light background.
- **Other components.** Here are several other elements worth testing:
  – 'Order Now' buttons
  – pictures of people
  – bio of yourself
  – headline colors
  – opening paragraph
  – bullet points (5 or 20?).

The key to seeing results is testing radically different variations. Don't test vanilla, French vanilla, and butter pecan … test vanilla, chili peppers and whisky! Once you start to notice an angle your prospects are responding to, refine your testing further. For example, if your headline 'Stop Making Bad Fried Chicken Now!' consistently outperforms the other variations, test it against a similar headline like 'Stop Making Bad Fried Chicken!' or 'Stop Frying Bad Chicken Now!'

Test an element until you have a consistent winner. After that, you should focus your efforts on a different element as there are serious diminishing returns. I prefer to set up large tests (i.e. a lot of variables) and let it run for a few months while I'm working on another project. This way, you are more likely to find a significant improvement, with minimal output.

Testing tools

Here's a short list of testing options:

- **Google Optimizer** (www.google.com/websiteoptimizer) – a free tool that can be used in conjunction with AdWords and Google Analytics. It is very easy to set up, does not require a host, and is loaded with tutorial videos. And did we mention that it was free? The downside is that it is a fully factorial experiment and will take a very, very, very long time to do multi-variable testing. For example, if you wanted to test three different headlines and three different logos, and received 100 visitors a day, it would take 77.7 days to conclude the test!
- **Kaizen Track** (www.kaizentrack.com) – a tool that we've used in the past with mixed success. It is installed on your server and is a very bare-bones application. If you are interested in Taguchi testing and are looking for a low-priced option, this certainly fits the bill.
- **Split Test Accelerator** (www.splittestaccelerator.com) – while we've never personally used this tool, we've heard nothing but good things about it. I've read quite a few articles by Dr James Stone, the creator of the STA, and have found him both knowledgeable and entertaining. The Split Test Accelerator offers several Taguchi tests (though not as many as Kaizen Track) and also many other features

such as the ability to test time on page and pay-per-click advertising. Dr Stone has created a fine product, but at $800 it may be a bit pricey to invest in for many online businesses. Dr Stone readily admits you should not purchase STA until your monthly revenue reaches $2,000.

- If you don't want to do the work yourself, hosted solutions include Optimost (www.optimost.com) and Verster (www.verster.com).

Autoresponders: never repeat yourself again

An autoresponder is a method of automatically e-mailing timed and customized messages at pre-determined intervals. It allows you to automatically follow up with your prospects indefinitely. Studies have shown that people must have seven points of contact before making a purchase, and on the web, you're lucky to get even one.

Here's the autoresponder process (Fig. 16):

- Sign up for autoresponder.
- They give you a code that creates an opt-in form.
- You put the code on your website.
- Visitors to your website sign up by including their e-mail address (and any other contact info you want to require).
- Their information gets stored online in the autoresponder database.
- You write messages online and determine when they should be sent out.

FIGURE 16 **AUTORESPONDER PROCESS**

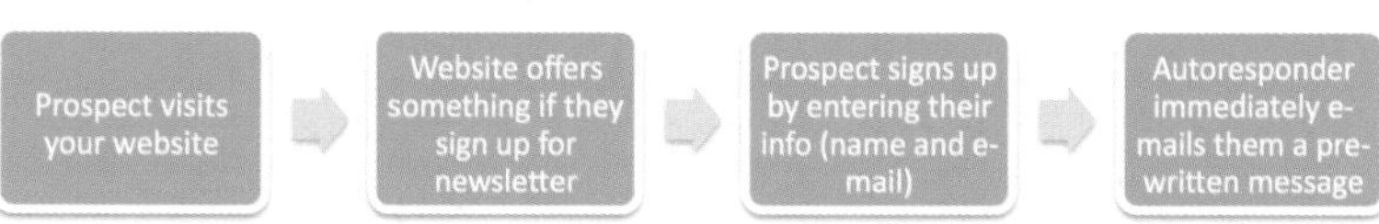
Prospect visits your website
Website offers something if they sign up for newsletter
Prospect signs up by entering their info (name and e-mail)
Autoresponder immediately e-mails them a pre-written message

In order to receive as many e-mail addresses from your visitors as possible, you need to offer something of value. This bears repeating, as so many people forget it: you will receive more opt-ins – and make more money – by offering real value.

REAL-LIFE EXAMPLE

One of our products wasn't selling well (a conversion rate of roughly 0.2%). Our advertisements were sending visitors to a sales page for a product that cost more than $100 / £65, a price that most people need time to mull over. We decided to change our strategy to build trust before going for the sale. Instead of sending visitors to a sales page, we directed them to a landing page – a customized web page that prospects 'land on' before they visit the home page/sales letter, which offered a free sample of the product if they signed up for our newsletter. It worked and more than 20% of visitors signed up. Let's highlight the advantages of this approach:

- Prospects now had an opportunity to test drive the product, building significant trust.
- Our sales drastically improved.
- I suddenly had a growing list of prospects to keep in touch with. I continued to write added-value e-mails, sprinkling in a few affiliate offers when applicable. This alone added an extra $80 / £50 a month – that's two days on Ko Phi Phi, Thailand – to our bottom line.

I wrote 14 follow-up messages for the autoresponder, each one sent about four days after the previous one. I haven't touched those messages in months and they are still being sent out to this day. If I do come across something the people on the newsletter list might find interesting, I let them know about it. When I recommend a product we invariably make a few sales.

It's important to note this wouldn't be possible without trust. I sign up for autoresponders all the time, just to see what other people are doing. I usually unsubscribe after the third or fourth message, because it's nothing more than thinly veiled sales pitches.

The ones I continue reading – and buying from – are informative pieces where I've gained an insight or valuable new resource. Perhaps the best newsletter I currently receive is written by Howie Jacobson, author of Google AdWords for Dummies. I open e-mails from him as quickly as I would from a friend or family member, reading each one just as carefully. When he does offer a product, it's highly relevant to my interests and at a good price.

Once your autoresponder has collected a few thousand leads, make sure to delete people who unsubscribed. Many autoresponders charge you for the total number of people on your list rather than the number of total subscribers. You should also split test messages that you send out to your subscribers, tracking which headlines result in a higher open rate and which copy leads to the most sales.

Check out more on autoresponders at:

- www.aweber.com
- www.getresponse.com

You can watch a video on how to set up an opt-in form on your website at www.stream-life.com.

Customer service

If you decide to follow a product development stream, customer service will grow increasingly important. If you want to sell ten products a month, you may only have to answer a few questions; if you're selling a thousand products a month, you need to build a stream that will handle the vast majority of customer questions and concerns automatically.

You will start to notice several recurring questions. Compile an ongoing list of these questions and create a frequently asked questions page on your website that addresses each one of these concerns. Make sure to link to this page from your sales page. This will help answer the majority of questions people have while on your website. This leaves you to answer the questions sent to you via e-mail.

To help automate this, you'll need to create two e-mail addresses. The first e-mail address will automatically reply with the list of frequently asked questions. At the bottom of the e-mail, be sure to include the second e-mail address that you or your customer service rep checks regularly.

Here's a copy of the e-mail I send out to my prospects:

> Hi
>
> Thank you for contacting us at <your autoresponder e-mail address>. This is an automatic response to let you know we have received your question. This e-mail address is used to send out lessons and newsletters to our subscribers and is not checked frequently. Do you have a question about <your product name>?
>
> I strive to deliver fast and honest answers to your questions. An answer today is better than tomorrow, so please try searching our growing knowledge base of frequently asked questions on <your product name>. Nearly all of our customers' questions are answered here.
> Just visit this link: <link to your FAQ page here>
>
> If the answer you're looking for could not be found on the Support Section, e-mail us at <your personal e-mail address> and one of our support staff members will get back to you as soon as possible.
>
> Get Answers Now At Our Support Section:
>
> <link to your FAQ page here>
>
> Best regards
>
> <name and website>

This setup lets your prospect receive an immediate response and frees you from answering the same questions over and over.

CUSTOMER SERVICE RESOURCES

Additional resources that will help you improve customer service:

Setting up your own toll-free number

- **Angel** (www.angel.com; tel. 1-888-692-6435). This service provides you with a toll-free number and call-forwarding to various departments (which may all be your cell phone at first).

- **Ring Central** (www.ringcentral.co.uk; tel. 1-888-898-4591). This is a similar service to Angel but with a stronger online presence.

Pay-by-minute call centers

If you need someone to answer phone calls for purchases and FAQs, these are your guys. Many people still feel uncomfortable purchasing online and just want to hear a voice on the other end. Give it to them, and collect your money!

- **West Teleservices** (www.west.com; tel. 1-800-232-0900)

- **Convergys** (www.convergys.com; tel. 1-888-284-9900)

Pay-by-commission

If you'd rather pay based on performance (i.e. offer a commission to salespeople) these are the ones to use.

- **InPulse** (www.inpulseresponse.com; tel. 1-800-841-9000)

THREE

Perspiration – Roadmap To Success and Adventure

By now you're probably anxious to put what you've learned into action. Below are three very different streams that will help fund your lifestyle. Choose the one that most interests you and get to work!

ROAD MAP 1: PRODUCT DEVELOPMENT STREAM

This is a step-by-step method for creating a downloadable or information product to sell online.

1. Research a niche you are interested in. Use WordTracker or the Google Keyword Tool to see how many people are looking for your topic. Try several variations such as 'fried chicken recipes,' 'fried chicken gravy recipes,' or 'boneless fried chicken recipes.'

2. Determine how many clicks you could realistically get per day. Use the Google Keyword Tool for this, though don't worry about their projected cost per click – it's almost always a gross overestimation.

3. Sign up for an autoresponder through Aweber. They have a money back guarantee, so if your test doesn't work, you don't pay.

4. Get a domain name and web hosting with BlueHost.

5. Create a simple three-page website. Check out our section on website development for more detailed information on how to do this. The three pages are:
   (a) **Sales page** – which includes a product picture, headline, as many benefits that your product provides as possible, a strong guarantee, a special bonus offer for buying today, and a call to action. Check out our section on sales letters.
   (b) **Order summary** – with a big button that says 'Yes! I Want (Your Product).' Once visitors click on that button, they can tentatively be called a sale.
   (c) **Sign-up page**, which has a simple line saying 'Sorry, our product is on backorder (or we are currently updating the product), please leave your name and e-mail and we will let you know when it is ready.' Those who leave their e-mail address are definitely considered sales. E-mail addresses that are left will be captured in your autoresponder for follow-up should you decide to launch.

6. Open a Google Analytics account and place tracking code on all three pages. This will allow you to track your visitors and see how many of them click through to each page. Be sure to add the third page as a Goal in Analytics, and give it the value of your product, minus payment processing. Add your IP address as a filter so your own clicks won't be added to the calculation (visit www.whatismyipaddress.com for your IP address). Check the Analytics Help Guide to learn more.

7. Create a Google AdWords campaign to drive traffic to your site.

8. Run your campaign for at least a week in order to reduce noise and inconsistencies. For example, let's say you run a campaign for three days before Christmas; do you really think those numbers will remain the same year round? At the end of the week tally the results. Assuming you are selling a digital product (which all beginners should) you can compare how much you spent on

advertising with how much revenue you would have made though your test sales by looking at the data in Google Analytics. If you are planning to sell a hard good like speakers or clothes, you have to factor in production costs as well. Take a long hard look at these numbers and decide whether it would be worth it to proceed. Pause all campaigns at the end of the test.

9. If your test shows a profit, roll up your sleeves and create your product. If it is information-based, you will be able to charge more by adding highly detailed, original content in different forms of media, such as audio and video.

   Be sure to include special bonus items to increase the value. You can do this by searching cNet for free programs you can sell, or look into public domain material on your topic. (You could also include another product you currently have, or create more content.) The best way to search for public domain material is to use those mentioned in the sections on the public domain or creative commons search (it's on the top right of your Firefox browser, as a drop-down menu). Be sure to check the boxes that allow you to modify the material for commercial purposes.

   When you launch your product, you have two options: the easy way, and the pro way. If you just want to get on with it, go ahead and launch your product. If you want to be a pro, set up a split test or Taguchi test for your sales page. Now when you launch, you will be testing variables from day one.

   Alternatively, you could set up a landing page that is designed to capture your prospects' e-mail addresses first and then follow up for a sale. Generally, this is a great strategy, as it gives you a chance to stay in contact with the prospect and recommend other products and/or services. Remember, you still have to provide value! Whichever direction you choose, it is wise to begin split testing. If testing the web pages themselves is too time-consuming initially, you can always split test your AdWords ads (which takes about 10 to 30 seconds to set up).

10. Set up a payment processor with PayPal and digital download processor with E-junkie if applicable.

11. Restart your Google AdWords campaign, and monitor your results in Google Analytics. Look at your AdWords campaign in Analytics, which gives two important metrics: cost-per-click (CPC) and return-per-click (RPC). This is a very simple way to see which keywords, ads and campaigns are making you money and which ones aren't. Continue to delete those that aren't making a profit while simultaneously testing your pages using Google Optimizer (http://www.google.com/websiteoptimizer). Gradually, your sales will increase and your advertising cost will decrease.

ROAD MAP 2: CONTENT-DRIVEN STREAM

This is a step-by-step method for creating a *content-driven stream* and making money from advertising and affiliates. Unlike Method 1, this requires very little start-up cost, but does take a lot of elbow grease. This is ideal for people who have more time than money. If you don't see yourself writing at least 30 articles, don't bother with this method. If you enjoy writing, this is a risk-free way to get your feet wet, and can be built into a solid business model that will last for years.

1. Research a niche you are interested in. Go to WordTracker and see how many people are looking for your topic. Try several variations such as 'fried chicken recipes,' 'fried chicken gravy recipes,' or 'boneless fried chicken recipes.'

Once you've decided there are people actually looking for these keywords, search the ClickBank Marketplace for products that you could sell. Attempt to negotiate a trial copy of the products, or just buy them. Try to choose three to five products, and write honest reviews about all of them.

2. Get a domain name and web hosting with BlueHost.
3. Sign up for an autoresponder through Aweber.
4. Write five short articles that offer tips about your niche (sample recipes for fried chicken, cooking methods, etc.). At the end of each article, give a quick background and recommend one of the products you signed up with from the ClickBank Marketplace. Make sure they are honest reviews.
5. Add those five articles to your website, each on its own page. We use Dreamweaver, but you can also download Nvu for free.
6. Sign up for Google AdSense and place their ads on each of those five pages.
7. Write five 'teasers' for those web pages, which will be emailed to your prospects every four days or so. They should offer a brief introduction like: 'Hi, I just created a new method of cooking fried chicken. You can check it out at www.friedchickengonewild.com/newcookingmethod.'
8. You could include the course directly into the e-mail though I prefer to send prospects to our website, for two reasons. First, you can include advertising on your site, which will bring in additional revenue. Second, your site will appear more valuable to the search engines (more content is always a good thing) and you will eventually start to see some traffic from search results.
9. Create a landing page that offers a five-day crash course in your niche. Visitors can access the course by signing up through Aweber. Now you have their e-mail address and can begin following up with them.

10. Register for an account with EzineArticles. At first, you are only allowed to submit ten articles at once, and they can take over a week to approve. Pick ten keywords that fit our search criteria (see the section on article marketing for an in-depth explanation) and write one article for each. Make sure to include the keyword in the title, a few times in the article, and once in the conclusion. Also, in your Bio box include a link to your site (preferably with the keyword as the link). A good way to get people to click on the link is to offer them a free report.

11. Submit all ten as soon as you finish them (the more quickly the better). After those ten are accepted, you will be able to submit 25 or an unlimited number, depending on how well your articles were written. Only after you've written 30 articles should you expect to see some money (not a lot, but some). Here is how the users' experience should play out:
    (a) They search for a keyword and click on your article in the search engine results.
    (b) They read your article and click on the link to your site.
    (c) They sign up for the free course and start receiving e-mails, with links to the course.
    (d) They read the teaser and click on the link.
    (e) On the web page, they either click on an AdSense ad (which pays you a few cents) or they purchase an affiliate product (which pays you dollars). Even if they don't do either of these (which most won't), they will receive another e-mail a few days later, and the process starts all over again.

12. Once you've set this up, use WordTracker and find dozens – if not hundreds — of keywords with at least ten daily searches and less than 1,000 competing sites. Write one article of 300 to 500 words that is highly optimized for each keyword and publish it to your website. Add the AdSense code and the occasional affiliate link where applicable. Be sure to include a sign-up form on each page offering your free course to capture leads and promote your products.

13. Create a site map using the Xml-Sitemap Generator and submit it to Google Webmaster Tools.

14. Purchase Backlink Builder (www.angelasdiscountmarket.com/backlink_builder.html) and start building 30 high PageRank links to your website. This will help you rise faster in the search engines. Outsource the link building by running an ad on Craigslist or Elance.

The beauty of this stream is that there is no financial risk. All you are paying for is the autoresponder and domain/host. The pros write hundreds of articles and drive huge amounts of traffic through this funnel, which can make a very nice income.

Profitable examples of a content-driven website are:

- www.Travel-smarts.com
- www.Seat61.com

You can see how I created a content-driven website at www.stream-life.com.

ROAD MAP 3: AFFILIATE NETWORK

You can generate traffic for this stream using search engine optimization and/or pay-per-click advertising. This stream does not require you to create any product, nor does it require you to create large amounts of content. However, it does require certain business and marketing skills, as you must find an underserved market, connect with numerous affiliates already servicing this market, and figure out a way to introduce the two so you can get paid. Here's how the stream works in detail:

1. When prospects arrive at your website for the first time, they are immediately greeted with your value proposition and an opt-in form in exchange for something of value. This could be a free e-book, audio course, or notifications of time-sensitive offers.
2. Once prospects subscribe, they continue to receive e-mails that either offer important information and/or pre-sales for affiliate products. Each e-mail contains a link to your website that has several related affiliate offers on it. For example, if you e-mail your prospects regarding vitamin supplements, you should send them to your web page that has several supplement offers. It's important to note that hyperbole does not get you very far in affiliate sales. Sure, you might make more money initially, but your unsubscribe rate will soar as prospects become increasingly disappointed in the products you promote.
3. The least expensive way to promote your site is article marketing. Open an account with EzineArticles and write dozens of articles geared toward your market. Be sure to optimize each article for a specific keyword that your market is searching for. This way, your articles will appear high in the search results for those phrases. Be sure to include the proper anchor text and links to your site, and highlight the free resource they'll receive for signing up.
4. Once you begin to see consistent revenue from this method, experiment with paid advertising methods. If you are able to generate a positive ROI, expand your campaigns. Test and refine them further yourself, or outsource the pay-per-click management to an expert.

The main advantage of this stream is that you do not have to supply customer support for the products as this responsibility falls squarely on the shoulders of the product developers. If you choose to stick with article marketing, your traffic generation requires no capital.

The downside of this stream is the lack of control. You don't own the rights to any of the products, nor do you control their sales letters. However, your website along with a well maintained autoresponder can remain a valuable asset for years to come.

An excellent example of this method can be found at www.moneymakingbuddy.com.

ADDITIONAL WAYS TO MAKE MONEY ONLINE

There are of course hundreds of other ways to produce income from the Internet. If marketing doesn't interest you, consider writing e-books for other sites that do the marketing for you and pay royalties of 30 to 50%.

You could work as a freelancer, offering your services and expertise where needed. While I tend to focus on building my own streams – and adhering to my 'get paid for the same work' axiom – I will occasionally act as a PPC consultant or teach a course at a local college. This keeps me sharp and provides additional revenue to support whatever I'm interested in at the time.

How about creating a forum about a topic you're passionate about? Once you reach a critical mass of users, start promoting products or accepting advertising.

Remember, it's not what you do – it's that you *do something*. The more you create, the more you make.

FOUR

Embarkation – You've Earned It

Congratulations! You've automated your income and freed up your time and location. Now it's time to start planning your dream trip.

While I worked as a travel agent, I would often take long walks, staring with envy at the airplanes arriving or departing from the airport. Granted, a lot of those people were flying for business, but dammit, they were going somewhere. Those airplanes provided a constant reminder of why Darcie and I built streams. We wanted to leave our home and explore the world, and we wanted to do so without worrying about financial responsibilities back home. On a cold January morning, we were the ones on that plane, headed to warmer climates.

The first part of this book requires ambition, hard work, and perseverance. Once your streams have begun to reach orbit, you'll need a whole new set of character traits as you begin your travels, namely patience, humility, and flexibility.

It would be beyond the scope of this book to provide advice on a specific location. Therefore, this section is about long-term travel in general, including advice on managing your streams while abroad.

The first part of this book is about what you can offer the world; this section pertains to discovering what the world can offer you.

Sit back, relax and enjoy. You've earned it.

PREPARING FOR LONG-TERM TRAVEL

Travelling abroad is an art. It requires intellect to plan, courage to enact, and perseverance to endure. When planning your dream trip, you must walk a fine line between over-analysis and not-so-blissful ignorance (summer in Sudan, anyone?).

There are several things you should consider *before* booking your travel, and the most important will be deciding *where and when to go*.

WHERE TO GO

After working in a cubicle and daydreaming about travelling around the world, most people already have a pretty good idea of where they want to go. It's a personal choice and there are amazing places to see and experience all over the globe. If you intend for your streams to pay for your travels, the main factor in deciding where to go is your budget.

MONEY

What your stream will make

If your very first stream is a smash hit, pulling in tens of thousands of dollars a month, the world is pretty much your oyster. However, the chances of that happening are slim to none and Slim just left town. Realistically, you can expect it to pull in between \$3 / £2 and \$10 / £7 a day at first, and expect higher earnings as you test and refine your streams. In order to help determine where you go, take a look at how much it will cost you per day.

How much the world costs

These numbers assume a few things. First, you travel slowly (no more than one out of every four days). Second, you stay in clean, basic accommodation. While it's certainly possible to rent a \$3 / £2 room in Cambodia, most people mature enough to run a business want a little more comfort. We're talking rooms with a bathroom, hot water, shower, towels, a bed, and a TV ... but not much else.

The prices below are costs per day and for two people and include food, room, laundry, toiletries, visas, and overland (usually local) travel:

- Southeast Asia: **$50 / £35**
- Australia and New Zealand: **$80 / £50**
- South America: **$55 / £35**
- Africa: **$60 / £40**
- Western Europe: **$90 / £60**
- Eastern Europe: **$65 / £43**
- Indian subcontinent: **$40 / £25**
- Japan: **$90 / £60**

As you can see, expenses can be fairly reasonable, far more reasonable than what you may be paying back home. However, you will want to travel somewhere that your streams can afford.

You can escape home faster and live better if you visit Third World areas such as Southeast Asia and India. There's another more powerful reason for going to the Third World initially: a new perspective. Chances are, if you're reading this you were probably raised in the Western world. When you board that plane, you will no doubt be ready for a change, and the transition from First World to Third World will be as eye-opening as the transition from worker to stream builder.

For more information on budgets for specific countries, visit http://www.solotravel.org/travel-budget-calculator.htm. This calculator allows you to adjust your budget according to accommodation preferences, street food versus restaurants, whether or not you use Internet cafes, and the number of drinks you have per day. Their calculations have been fairly close to my personal experiences.

Money-saving tips

Here are some tips I've learned from working as a travel agent and through personal experience. There are many, many ways to stretch your budget.

- **Purchase tickets ahead of time, or last minute.** My golden rule of travel: if you have concrete dates (such as weddings) you will save yourself a bundle by purchasing tickets as far in advance as possible. If you are flexible, wait until the last minute and choose your destination by price.
- **Slum it, then go all out.** Darcie and I cycled across Ireland without breaking the bank, and yet we stayed in quality bed and breakfasts (including an old Irish castle). How did we do this? Simple: for every one night in a great location, we camped two nights. Once we arrived at our room for the night, we cleaned up and had a good time. The next morning we showered and hit the road. Following this approach you only miss a shower for one day at a time …
- **Change your drinking habits.** One of my largest grievances with budget travel writers is their silly notion that you should sacrifice a cold beer in the name of saving money. There are far better ways to save money while you're travelling. What you *should* avoid are bars. You can drink cold beer or local spirits for cheap from bottle shops (or, oddly enough, 7-Elevens). I found myself contemplating buying a can of Guinness in Thailand for more than it cost back home! True, it was an Irish pub on St Patrick's Day, but come on.

A real-life example

When I send e-mails back home to friends, the most common response goes something like 'I'd love to travel to ______________, but I can't because of lack of money/lack of time.' From Chapters 2 and 3 on Education and Perspiration you've learned how to create streams that free up your time while providing income to help you enjoy life – but how much income is needed to fund world travel? In order to address this common concern, let's take a look at my personal world travel statistics.

First, a brief background on our world travels adventure. Darcie and I took a year off and moved from our townhouse outside of San Francisco to Southeast Asia. From there we traveled though Thailand,

Cambodia, Malaysia, Vietnam and Indonesia before heading to India and Nepal. After a month of trekking in Nepal we caught a train to Beijing, then the Trans-Mongolian Railway to Europe before flying home. We bought three plane tickets: San Francisco to Bangkok, Bangkok to Mumbai, and Frankfurt to San Francisco. All other travel was by boat, rail, or bus.

Here are our world travel statistics for both of us:

- **Average monthly living expenses: $1,300 / £860.** This included staying in moderately priced hotels and eating street food half of the time, with the occasional big night out. We didn't really drink that much at bars, which would have driven our costs up significantly (for some reason, a beer in a bar can cost more than a bed in some parts of the world).
- **Visa requirements: $80 / £50 per month.** Our first month in Thailand was free, while the month in Nepal was $80 /£50 plus $20 / £15 for entry into the Everest region.
- **Total for three flights (both of us): $2,700 / £1,780.** In retrospect, we could have gotten a better deal if we had booked ahead, but we honestly did not know where we were headed.
- **Total for train travel: $2,000 / £1,320.** Over half of this was for the Trans-Mongolian, which considering we crossed eight time zones wasn't a bad deal.
- **Total cost for our round-the-world travel adventure?** This came to $21,260 – about the same as if we had stayed at home.

By hitting the road, our streams paid for everything. Had we stayed at home we would have had to keep our jobs. We hope this helps inspire your next big trip.

SAFETY

Safety is a big concern for travellers. What they fail to realize is that they are no more likely to injured or worse on the road than back home. It all comes down to being aware of your surroundings and making smart decisions.

For more information on travel warnings, visit the *US Department of State Worldwide Travel Warnings* at http://travel.state.gov.

While travel warnings don't really deter Darcie and I from travelling, we do stick to common sense advice such as:

- Don't carry a wallet or purse, use a money belt.
- Don't get drunk and walk around at night.
- Don't sleep in public places.
- Don't attract attention to yourself or your belongings.
- Try not to look like a lost tourist.
- Trust your gut instincts.

GETTING THERE AND GETTING AROUND

Round-the-world (RTW) plane tickets

Round-the-world travel packages can be the single best way to see the world. I have known many people who have taken the plunge (and have had the pleasure myself), and must say it's not only a great way to save money, it's a life-changing event.

The most common round-the-world tickets (RTW) are offered through airlines or specialty providers such as Airtreks.com. By purchasing an RTW, you get to visit five to ten destinations for the price of two or three. When I was a student I travelled through Sydney, Singapore, Vietnam, Nepal, London, Toronto, and San Francisco for less than $1,300 / £860 (granted, this was in 2000, so don't expect a deal that good).

The beauty of RTW tickets is that many of them offer stopovers in countries you weren't to visit, affording you the opportunity to see more of the world for less. On my first trip I hadn't intended to visit Singapore, but since I had a free stopover, why not?

If you have budgetary concerns, stick to major cities. The main hubs for round-the-world travel packages tend to be San Francisco, Los Angeles, New York, London, Frankfurt, Singapore, Bangkok, and Sydney. Australia in general is a standard inclusion in a round-the-world ticket, and provides you the option to travel without flying from northern Oz to East Timor, Indonesia, and Southeast Asia.

Additional cities to consider are Barcelona, Delhi, Mumbai, Auckland, and Paris. Notice that Africa and South America are completely left out? For some reason, adding these continents can really drive up the price of round-the-world travel tickets. A few notable exceptions are Rio de Janeiro, Buenos Aires, and Johannesburg, South Africa.

The bottom line is that if you plan to spend a significant amount of time abroad (i.e. more than five months) *and* want to see more of the world for less, think about purchasing a round-the-world ticket. You can find cheap multi-destination flights for the same price as a round trip.

If you are interested in purchasing a return ticket only, look into buying a wholesale ticket from airline consolidators.

Discount plane tickets

Airline consolidators

Airline consolidators provide some of the greatest deals on international tickets. Rather than buying an RTW ticket, which limits your flexibility, you can purchase an *open jaw ticket* – an airplane ticket that arrives in one city and departs from another. If you intend to travel overland, this option will provide more flexibility and *may* actually be cheaper in the long run.

So how do airline consolidators work? Generally, they purchase large amounts of tickets to cover the world's most popular routes, which they then resell to travel agents and the general public. Bear in mind, however, that many tickets purchased through consolidators are non-refundable and may have high change fees.

Here's a short list of airline consolidators I've used in the past:

- Skylink: www.skylinkus.com/
- C&H: www.cnhintl.com/
- cFares: www.cfares.com/
- Flight Centre: www.flightcentre.co.uk

Low-cost airlines

While I'm a strong advocate of overland travel, flying not only can save you time (flying to Lukla from Kathmandu can save a week's trekking in the Himalaya), it can also be cheaper. Thanks to the introduction of local low-cost providers around the world, travellers are finding it easier – and more economical – than ever to see more of the world.

Here is a list of low-cost airlines that can save you a bundle:

- Priceline: www.priceline.com – make use of the bidding feature for true bargain hunting.
- cFares: www.cfares.com – well known for providing consolidator rates for international flights – as a travel agent, I used them a lot.
- 1-800-FLY-EUROPE: www.1800flyeurope.com.
- Discount airlines for flights within Europe: www.ryanair.com; www.easyjet.com.
- Discount airlines for flights within Asia: www.airasia.com.
- Round the world specialists: www.airtreks.com

Air passes

Air passes are a great alternative if you need to cover a lot of ground quickly. Air passes are offered by airlines, or the alliance they belong to, and offer deep discounts for multi-segment flights within a given region. Remember, while they provide cheap tickets, most air passes come with a lot of restrictions, though most can be changed if need be.

A caveat: air passes must be purchased outside the region in which you intend to travel. For example, Asian air passes cannot be purchased in Asia.

Check out http://airtimetable.com/airpass.htm for a complete, up-to-date listing of air passes around the world.

Train passes

Train passes are a great way to see more of the countryside and save money at the same time. While generally good value, train passes are usually purchased for a specific period of time, meaning the pass is cheaper the more you travel during that period. As you probably realize, I'm not a proponent of travelling fast, which is a serious downside to train passes. However, they do save you the hassle of fighting through ticket lines – especially in India — as they move you to the front of the line.

Check out www.seat61.com for the most up-to-date information about long-distance international train travel.

HEALTH: AVOIDING PROBLEMS

Vaccinations

You need to start getting some of your vaccinations at least two months before departing on a trip. Several inoculations require three or four visits, spaced two to three weeks apart. Here's a short list of the most common vaccinations required (or highly recommended) for global travel:

- hepatitis A and B (if possible, get the combined vaccine)
- Japanese encephalitis
- polio, diphtheria and tuberculosis

- rabies
- tetanus
- typhoid
- yellow fever.

Malaria

While there is no vaccination for malaria, there are a number of anti-malarial tablets you can take to help combat the disease (though none of them is 100% effective). Check with your doctor to see which prescription is right for you. You can also learn more at www.malaria.org.

To get these vaccinations, visit your local travel clinic or speak with your doctor. If you're currently employed, check if your benefits will cover the cost of vaccinations. I was able to save more than $700 / £460 in the States on vaccinations thanks to the health insurance provided by my previous employer. Talk about a severance package!

Food

When it comes to food, I follow a few simple rules:

1. Eat at restaurants with a lot of people and high turnover. It probably means the food is fresher.

2. Eat cooked food. Try to avoid any raw vegetables and raw fish. Fruits and vegetables that you can peel are a safer option. Consider bringing vitamin tablets if you're not getting enough fruits and vegetables.

3. Don't overeat. If you stuff your face with contaminated food, you'll feel a helluva lot worse than if you ate a smaller portion. The only two times I've been sick abroad were shortly after a three- or four-course meal at an upmarket steakhouse.

Water

Depending on where you travel, you might need to take a water purification system. I use the Steripen Adventurer UV purifier. The same size as a screwdriver, this wonder tool can purify a liter of water in one minute using an ultraviolet light bulb and lithium batteries. Though it isn't cheap – retail is about $130 / £85 – the Steripen is both lightweight and effective. Bear in mind it doesn't work with ice, a common cause of getting sick among travellers.

If you're planning to buy bottled water overseas, bear in mind that many merchants refill used water bottles with local water and resell them. If the plastic seal is broken — and it often is – you probably don't want to drink it.

Traveller's diarrhea

Traveller's diarrhea claims 30 to 50% of tourists abroad within the first two weeks, and is often accompanied by vomiting. In other words, don't be surprised if you're leaking out both ends … it's natural. The best thing to do? Take over-the-counter anti-diarrheal medicine or antibiotics (rather than something that just plugs you up), drink lots of water, lay low and let the good – or bad – times flow. The symptoms should clear up within a few days. Any more than that, contact a doctor.

VISAS

Think flights are boring? Try deportation

A true story: when I was 20 years old, I purchased a round-the-world ticket originating in Australia, flying to Vietnam (Saigon), with a layover in Singapore. The travel agent who sold me the ticket failed to mention that American citizens must have a visa to enter Vietnam.

After flying into Ho Chi Minh airport, I learned first-hand that American citizens *do* in fact need a visa. About five minutes after getting off the plane, I was sent back to Singapore without a Vietnamese stamp in my passport. It was a pretty embarrassing experience. On a good note, I finally made it back to Vietnam years later with visa in hand.

Visa requirements

Many countries require you to apply for a travel visa simply to enter. Think of it as a cover charge, and when you consider that it costs less to enter Vietnam than a swanky nightclub in New York, it doesn't seem so bad.

In order to ensure you don't have your own deportation story, follow these tips:

- **Contact your local embassy.** Government website travel sections provide the most up-to-date information on visa requirements, including fees, limitations, and which type of visa is right for you (student, tourist, business, immigrant, etc.).
- **Have headshots of yourself (passport-size and in colour).** If you plan to obtain a visa on the road, some countries will require you to provide a headshot of yourself. Before you leave for your big trip, bring least two passport-size colour photos for each country you plan to visit. This way you won't have to pay big bucks or run around trying to get them at the last minute.
- **Note the differences between tourist and business visas.** Business visas are much more difficult to obtain than a tourist visa. A client of mine could not fly to Brazil because he was flying for business purposes. After going back and forth with the visa department, which said the application would take weeks to process, we finally applied for (and received) a tourist visa in a few days, allowing him to make his meeting.
- **Be prepared for bureaucracy.** When applying for a visa, remember, you are dealing with governments. God help you. There will be fees, delays, 'special' conditions ... be prepared, and plan ahead to prevent these unavoidable events from delaying your trip.

- **Purchase travel visas prior to arrival.** To determine whether or not you need a travel visa, check your country's embassy site, which provides a full listing of travel visa requirements, as well as any time limitations on your visit. This was the most obvious lesson learned from my adventure in Vietnam. I made sure to obtain a Nepalese visa before flying to Kathmandu on the next segment. The funny thing is, some countries allow you to purchase travel visas at the border while some do not. Take my advice: don't chance it.

TYING UP LOOSE ENDS

Before you hit the road you'll need to close up shop. While most of these steps aren't necessary for short-term travel, they are imperative for long-term wandering.

- **Three to six months out:**
  - Get a passport.
  - Book your airplane flights.
  - Visit your doctor or travel clinic to get vaccinations. Check if your employer's health insurance covers them before you quit!
  - Determine how to handle your living situation. Consider renting out your residence furnished. This saves you the hassle of storing your belongings and moves you one step closer to paying off your mortgage. Most people interested in furnished accommodation are working abroad for a year or more – perfect for your intentions.
  - Book appointments with a dentist, doctor, and optometrist one month before you go to make sure you have a clean bill of health. This gives you time to handle any problems before you leave.

- **One month out:**
  - Set cancellation dates for all insurance policies, credit cards, and other miscellaneous items.
  - Close any unnecessary accounts (e.g. bank accounts and department store accounts).
  - Sign up for online banking.

  - Set up a forwarding address with the post office (a friend or a PO box in your name).
  - Find someone to rent your car while you're gone. Draft an automobile leasing contract and make sure the renter gets insurance.
  - Go to your dentist, doctor, and optometrist appointments.
  - Get travelers' insurance.

- **Two weeks out:**
  - Give your two weeks' notice to your employer.
  - E-mail yourself copies of your passport, driver's license, insurance policy, credit card, and any other important information you might need while you're away.
  - Get traveler's checks and e-mail the security numbers from those to yourself.
  - Notify your bank that you'll be making purchases in a foreign country with your credit card.
  - Have a garage sale. If you don't manage to sell the majority of your belongings, have another garage sale the following week. Darcie and I made more than $1,500 / £990 for two days spent selling our stuff – worth more than a month of travel in Southeast Asia. If you can't sell your stuff, look into a storage unit.
  - Get a visa, if applicable, for your first country.

Remember, you don't need half of what you may think you do, a truism that applies to a crucial step in preparing: packing for long-term travel.

WHAT (NOT) TO PACK

Prior to departure: create a checklist of items you need to take. At a *maximum* you should include:

- Passport
- Driver's license (international if possible)
- Airline/train tickets
- Credit cards, travelers' checks and US dollars

- Photocopies of important documents
- Youth hostel card
- Scuba diving certification (if applicable)
- Passport photos (2 per country)
- Money belt
- One small day pack
- A good book
- Pen and notepad
- Laptop and headset for Skype
- Two pairs of lightweight pants
- One pair of shorts
- Three shirts (one for going out)
- One pair of sandals
- One pair of shoes *or* boots
- Underwear
- Swimsuit (if applicable)
- Toiletries
- Silk sleep sack (not a sleeping bag)
- Sewing kit
- Nail clippers
- Earplugs
- First-aid kit
- Swiss army knife
- Watch
- Sunglasses

Possessions will only tie you down. For example, let's say you purchase a brand new digital camera before your trip (chances are you will). Sure, it's a great way to document your experiences, but it weighs you down a lot more than you think.

You have to think twice about swimming in the ocean for fear someone will steal it. Crossing a river could potentially destroy it. Strangers become potential threats. Worse than this though, it prevents you from truly experiencing a place before reaching for your camera. This effectively removes you from your surroundings, preventing you from ever really gaining anything at all.

OK, that's the end of my Taoist rant.

When travelling long term, minimalism is key. There's no sense packing everything you think you might need when you can always buy extras along the way as needed. Besides, navigating foreign markets is a highlight on many itineraries ... why not buy something there you might actually need?

Remember: pack light and stay flexible!

GUIDEBOOKS: EAT, SLEEP, AND LIVE LIKE THE TOURISTS

As for guidebooks, I tend to use them sparingly. Anyone who has done extensive travelling can attest it's very easy to find yourself inadvertently hitched to the Lonely Planet trail. The sad thing – which Lonely Planet readily admits – is that a guesthouse's quality will decline after a write-up in a popular guidebook. With guaranteed steady traffic from the guidebooks, the proprietors don't have to work as hard (kinda like you and your streams). This means you may be led exactly where you *don't* want to go.

Guidebooks are, however, great for planning a general route. When exploring a region, I often read about a country other than the one I'm in. It's better to use guidebooks that cater to your specific interests. For example, if you're looking for some creature comforts, avoid the budget travel guidebooks like the Lonely Planet *On A Shoestring* series.

If forced to choose one, Rough Guides would be my guidebook of choice. Their information is much more concise, with budget recommendations that are spot on. Lonely Planet tends to be off the mark when describing certain locations and uses too many adjectives for my taste. Don't paint me a picture of where I'm headed; just tell me what to expect.

While you can purchase guidebooks before you leave, you will often find free copies left behind by travellers. It makes sense – travellers generally arrive and depart from the same areas, and those leaving have no use for that guidebook anymore. Make sure to pass it on when you leave!

Free travel guides abound, thanks to the Internet. While they may not be as robust as a Lonely Planet or Rough Guide book, online travel guides can give you more information in less time. On my last trip to Southeast Asia, I didn't even bother with a book … all the intelligence I needed was on one site.

Here's a list of where you can find (mostly) free international travel guides:

- **Travelfish.org.** Far and away my favorite site on Southeast Asia. Travelfish covers Thailand, Laos, Vietnam, and Cambodia in great detail, and is expanding to Malaysia and Singapore. What I love about this site is its ability to convey information you need in the shortest amount of time: its navigation is simply brilliant, and anyone looking to learn more about these countries should check it out.
- **Lonelyplanet.com/thorntree/.** A forum offshoot of Lonely Planet, this is a great place to ask questions and get answers from people that are travelers, not tourists. Have a concern about a specific area? Visa requirements unclear? Are those laws really enforced, or can you bribe your way through it? Run it up the thorn tree and find out. I have heard whispers in this forum that Lonely Planet is planning to launch a buy-what-you-want program, where people can purchase only certain parts of a guidebook at a fraction of the cost. Check out their site to learn more (www.lonelyplanet.com/thorntree/).
- **Bootsnall.com.** A site loaded with international travel guides, focusing mainly on Europe. There are also great interviews, pictures, and fellow travellers' tales to share.

In my opinion, these are the three best places online to find cheap or free international travel guides, and I have used all three with great success.

WHY EINSTEIN WAS WRONG – HOW TO TRAVEL

The theory of relativity states that time slows down as speed increases. For example, imagine a friend whizzing across our solar system in a spacecraft while you remain here on the Earth. Einstein proved that your friend's clock would seem to tick more slowly than your own.

Sadly, the opposite is true when travelling. People who travel near the speed of light – or at least sound – arrive home seemingly unaware of where they have just visited. Locations become nothing more than a check box on their itinerary, an experience not to be savored but shown off to others. They develop the classic 'If it's Tuesday, this must be Rome' syndrome. Speed is not better, which is why you shouldn't try to travel at the speed of light.

My advice is to travel at the speed of smell.

As I write this, there is a large Vietnamese market going on less than five meters away. The smell of *pho* boiling over and the sounds of locals conversing is something I wouldn't have noticed on a five-day whirlwind tour of Vietnam.

In order to really experience your surroundings, you must slow down. While guidebooks may offer walking tours that allow you to 'do' a city in a day, it takes much longer to 'feel' it.

Somewhere along the line, we lost the point of travel. People visit pagodas, temples, churches, museums, and art galleries, not out of personal interest, but out of some misplaced obligation. If you aren't interested in art, skip the Museum of Modern Art. If you don't like sports, forget the Superdome. Can't stand witnessing first-hand poverty? Don't go to India.

It's not about seeing the most acclaimed sights. It's about *experiencing those that affect you the most.*

YOUR FIRST NIGHT ABROAD: MAKE IT A SOFT LANDING

Your first two days in any new region should be seen as a transition period. Don't throw yourself into the mix right away; book your hotel prior to departure and stay there for at least two nights. This will help you acclimatize to your new surroundings and sleep comfortably for the first few days. Your first few nights shouldn't be concerned with travel plans, budgets, or any other logistics ... just unplug and rest while your body adapts to the new sights, smells, and time zone.

LUNCH AT 4 A.M.? HOW TO DEAL WITH JET LAG

There are several ways to combat jet lag, a common problem among travelers. It certainly hits some people harder than others. It takes me more than a week to adjust, while Darcie takes changing time zones in her stride. Here are some ways to battle jet lag:

- **Don't eat.** Studies have shown that your liver takes longer to adapt to a new time zone than any other part of your body. By not eating for 12 hours or more, your body will adjust much more quickly. If this seems like too much, try eating on your intended destination's clock a few days before departure (dinner at 10 a.m., anyone?).
- **Sunshine.** The sun helps you set your circadian clock, so the more the better. Exercise also helps.
- **Pop some pills.** There are over-the-counter pills that claim to help with jet lag. Though I have no personal experience with them, several people I've spoken to swear by No-Jet-Lag.

REAL-WORLD EXPERIENCE: THIRD WORLD ECONOMICS AT WORK

Front-end and back-end offers don't just apply to the Internet; you can find them in a variety of markets. For example, say you're trying to find a guesthouse to stay in while travelling in India. Somebody shows you your room, which you decide is a good place to stay, but feel you can negotiate the price down a bit. You offer to pay 70% of the asking price in exchange for committing to a four-night stay. The owner is willing to offer a discount on the front end, in the hope they'll make it up on the back end. After all, many people who stay at the guesthouse also eat there, use the Internet, request laundry services, purchase water, etc.

Keep this in mind when dealing with your customers and prospects. Depending upon your offer, you may end up making more money on the back and then on the front end. This is why so many people give away free offers, courses, and e-books online. By giving something away for free on the front end, they invariably build trust with their prospects and improve their sales – not to mention ROI – by selling the products at a later date on the back end.

RESOURCES

- **Escape Artist** (www.escapeartist.com). Seeing that I write for them, it's kind of obvious to list them as a resource, huh? Honestly, Escape Artist is *the* place for advice on moving and investing abroad.
- **Outside Magazine** (http://outside.away.com). This is the inspiration station, with top-notch travel writers spinning narratives that will have you racing to the airport.
- **Lonely Planet: The Thorn Tree** (www.lonelyplanet.com/thorntree/). This forum is full of seasoned vets willing to offer advice on an amazingly wide variety of topics. It was here that I first learned that Vietnam no longer charged a departure tax at its airports (the tax is now included in the ticket price).

- **Family Travel Forum** (www.familytravelforum.com). *The* place for family travel advice.
- **Round-The-World FAQ** (www.perpetualtravel.com/rtw). This is one of the few travel books I have read cover to cover. This FAQ examines issues such as travel insurance, transport options, and travel with children in exhaustive detail.
- **US Centers for Disease Control and Prevention** (www.cdc.gov/travel). The definitive site for up-to-date info on what vaccinations are needed. Keep in mind that some countries require proof of immunization (usually yellow fever) before allowing you to enter. If you are currently employed, see if your insurance will cover your shots. Otherwise, they could cost between $500 / £300 and $1,000 / £660.
- **Tax planning** (www.irs.gov/publications/p54/). This will come into play. Make sure you have an accountant back home who is well versed in business and international tax planning. Set up this relationship before you go, and provide him or her with power of attorney so they can deal with things on your behalf.
- **Global Freeloaders** (www.globalfreeloaders.com). An essential resource for those looking to immerse themselves in a new culture. This site connects travellers with open-minded hosts who offer free housing. Just be sure to reciprocate when you get home!
- **The Couchsurfing Project** (www.couchsurfing.com). A very good friend of ours used this non-profit website to secure free accommodations in Puerto Rico for one week. The host took her out snorkeling, to his favorite restaurants, and to some of his favorite live bands. Highly recommended.

85

Tying It All Together

Travelling around the world is a difficult concept for most folks to grasp. While a dream for many, it seldom enters the realm of possibility. Convincing your friends and family that you want to leave your existing life behind is hard enough, but explaining your intention to make a living without working will probably fall upon deaf ears.

Express your travel intentions as soon as possible to allow friends and family time to come around. Eventually, they'll be just as excited about your trip as you are. If you are only making enough money to support your travels – rather than live like a millionaire back home – then consider downplaying your business-building (or don't mention it at all). Remember …

Just because money's coming in, that doesn't make you rich
Automated income can make you feel like a rock star, and travelling in the Third World allows you to party like one. Still, a healthy shot of reality may be needed. While you may be able to travel the world on the income your streams provide, that's a long way from paying for a similar lifestyle back home. We're from the San Francisco Bay Area, and are still a long way from the standard of living we enjoy abroad.

The purpose of creating streams is the freeing up of time and location. As you continue to develop more, you will eventually equal – and surpass – the income levels of your friends back home.

With that in mind, it's in your best interest to travel sooner than later. We left the country when our business generated $1,300 / £890 per month on autopilot. That wasn't enough money to quit our jobs and stay home … but it was more than enough to scuba dive Ko Lanta in Thailand, ride bicycles around Angkor Wat in Cambodia, trek up to Mount Everest Base Camp, sunbathe on world-class beaches in East Timor, get drunk with the Vietnamese locals on Bia Hoi ('draught beer') and take cooking classes in India. In other words, *if we made more money we wouldn't have lived so richly.*

While we do miss our loved ones (and Mexican food), seeing the world sure beats sitting on a couch back home. Besides, your loved ones can always come out and visit …

Visitors: budget ahead

Hopefully, you will have friends and family willing to fly halfway around the world for a visit. Unfortunately, they are coming with a very different mindset: whereas you are time-rich, they are time-starved, and willing to spend copious amounts of money on their one- or two-week vacation. Your daily budget – at one time very comfortable – feels like a mere pittance when your loved ones arrive ready to live it up.

Don't be a killjoy. You know they're coming, so budget accordingly. If you tend to live on \$50 / £35 per day, scale back to around \$30 / £20 a week before and a week after their visit (eat cheaper meals, go on long walks, read more, etc.). Darcie and I spend several hundred dollars more than usual whenever we have visitors, and thanks to planning ahead, the experiences we share are enriching, not impoverishing. Budgeting before and after will spread out your sacrifices and will help you appreciate your time with loved ones all the more. Now, pass the Cristal …

YOU CAN LEARN A LOT FROM A DIVE MASTER

My wife and I recently went diving off the coast of Thailand. Thirty meters underwater I flailed my arms in an attempt to swim around coral reefs, while the dive master glided effortlessly through the water. It took a while to realize how futile my efforts were. You can steady yourself very easily by pressing a button on your buoyancy control (known as a BC). I was wasting a lot of energy trying to stay still – when all I had to do was press a button, relax, and breathe.

Your streams are the same way. Many people starting out suffering from 'paralysis by analysis,' a reasonable though time-consuming urge to understand everything before taking a single step. The key to successful stream building is balancing your knowledge with taking appropriate action. Rather than waving your arms around and getting nowhere, concentrate on core objectives that will keep you afloat.

STAYING CONNECTED

Now that you've freed up your time and location, you'll need to monitor your streams and stay in touch with loved ones. Here are several crucial tools to maintain your streams abroad.

Poste Restante

A great way to pick up care packages from home. Get the address of the main post office in whatever town you're in (or will be shortly) and have people address your mail to the following:

LAST NAME, First Name
Poste Restante, General Post Office
Town, Country

When you arrive at the post office, simply present your passport as identification and you'll be able to claim your mail. Generally post offices around the world will hold mail for up to two years.

Blog

You can keep in touch by starting a travel blog. Blogger.com or WordPress.com are both free and can be set up in minutes. By creating a travel blog, you are able to avoid sending out group e-mails, which always come across as forced and rather generic. This way, people who were really interested in your trip can check up on you whenever they like, leave comments, and engage other people visiting your blog.

Also, blogs allow you much more creative freedom than sending e-mails. You can include pictures, video, polls, international clocks, maps, and a whole host of other customizations, all of which provide a great scrapbook after your travels.

Word of the year: wi-fi

Wireless is the name of the game. As time progresses, connecting to the Internet will only become increasingly important, so you might as well get used to ranking 'free Internet' higher than amenities such as free breakfast, swimming pool, and massages. Let's face it, you're now able to create streams that pay for your lifestyle, completely free of employees. Free of fax machines, cubicles, commutes, and water coolers … so logging into your accounts to make sure the money's coming in doesn't seem like too much of a hindrance, does it?

Expect Internet cafes to run to around \$1 / £0.65 to \$2 / £1.30 an hour. Seeing that your business is Internet-based, you may want to consider travelling with a laptop depending upon your goals.

Laptop: luxury or necessity?

If you intend to develop more streams while travelling, a laptop is necessary. You will need to upload web pages to your sites, conduct phone interviews with prospective freelancers, and keep tabs on your expenses and revenue streams. If you intend to just monitor or expand your existing streams, you can use Internet cafes, though working amid Chinese computer gamers ain't what it's cracked up to be.

Laptops also provide more security. You don't know what kind of spyware (programs that remember your keystrokes for future use) might be on some random computer. To paraphrase sex ed teachers, a trusting, monogamous relationship is one of the best ways to avoid viruses.

Mobile phone

Though I personally don't use one, the mobile phone service is getting better all the time, and can save you a lot of time if you need to call people who don't use Skype. For example, I spent 30 minutes in search of an international phone to make a two-minute call to my bank.

Skype

You can't go wrong with free international phone calls, and Skype provides just that. Get your friends and family back home to sign up and you can chat through your laptop for free. More businesses are jumping on the bandwagon, though banks and credit card companies are still lagging behind.

An additional feature that may be of some use is the ability to forward calls from a domestic phone number to your mobile phone abroad. If you handle customer service questions, it pays to list a domestic number. After all, would you buy a product from a company that requires you to call East Timor with questions?

Dragon Naturally Speaking

If it wasn't for this software, this book would never have been written. For a modest amount you get a microphone, headset, and the ability to dictate to your laptop. I'm able to 'write' at about 120 words per minute. An added bonus is that you can use the microphone and headset with Skype.

USB card/storage device card

An absolutely essential tool. There will be times when you won't be able to access the Internet with your laptop, and a handy USB or storage device allows you to back up your work.

Other technological marvels for working abroad

- **GoToMyPC** (www.gotomypc.com). This software allows you to access your home computer from any other computer in the world. If you object to travelling with a laptop, this is the way to go. Just remember, you'll have to pay for Internet connection along the way, making this a better solution for short-term travel.

- **World Electronics USA** (www.worldelectronicsusa.com). Get information on global phones. Provides a good explanation of which GSM frequencies and 'bands' function in which countries, which will determine the phone you purchase for travel (and perhaps home).
- **Universal Plug Adapter** (www.franzus.com). I've purchased adapters in several countries to power our digital camera and laptop, though it can be a hassle if you're exploring several different regions. This universal adapter works wonders around the world.
- **World Electric Guide** (www.kropla.com). This site is a lifesaver when it comes to handling electronics abroad. It breaks down voltage, wattage, and a slew of other technical requirements by country.

Working offline

There are several tools available that will help you work offline the majority of the time. For example, you can use Google AdWords Editor to manage your AdWords campaigns from your desktop and upload the changes whenever you have an available Internet connection.

Dragon Naturally Speaking can be used with Microsoft Word to dictate and edit sales letters, autoresponder e-mails, and article marketing submissions. Just be careful to copy and paste your work into a text file (.txt.) before adding it to your site, as Microsoft Word does not translate easily into HTML.

You can also save some of your most visited web pages onto your desktop.

OUTSOURCING

Employees: the only thing worse than being one is having one

The mere idea of employing someone makes me shiver. While I have a team of people who handle various aspects of our streams, none are employed by me. They are paid as consultants to do specific tasks.

It would be presumptuous to think I could create enough work for someone to occupy half their waking hours. I'm not paying for people; I'm paying for minds, hands, eyes, and brains. No one is essential to my streams, not even myself. That was the whole point: to create a stream that can handle nearly all aspects of our business without bothering anyone.

TEACH A MAN TO FISH ... AND HE'LL LEAVE YOU ALONE

As the captain, your main role in your streams is a creative one. You must create new ideas and scale them up. A student of mine was running in circles answering the same questions from prospects when all he needed was to create an online FAQ and set up an autoresponder campaign.

Remember the adage 'Give a man a fish and feed him for a day; teach a man to fish and feed him for a lifetime.' You must teach your streams to run on their own, otherwise you will find yourself doing the same work over and over.

Focus on core, outsource everything else

If your streams aren't moving forward as planned, it's up to you to do something about it. Of course, your streams should handle most issues without a hitch, but tasks such as answering unique prospect questions and handling refunds are not the most efficient uses of your time.

Outsource any aspect of your business that is simple, time-consuming, or painful for you to do. While I enjoy conducting SEO research, I hate building links and submitting sites to directories.

Therefore this is the first thing I outsource, as it requires no thought whatsoever, but is highly important to the success of our streams. Once a website is generating at least $50 / £35 per month, I pay a freelancer to build 30 new high PageRank links per month (using Backlink Builder for $5 / £3.50) to the site, using specific anchor text whenever possible. Here is the advertisement I posted on Craigslist and Elance, which works like a charm:

CLICK AND GET PAID: NO EXPERIENCE NEEDED

We need to hire someone on a monthly basis to add links to our two websites. This will help move our websites up in the search engines, making it easier for people to find us. Trust me – this is easier than it sounds. We will provide you with a document that includes step-by-step instructions (including screenshots) on how to add the links to our websites on 30 other websites. It will involve:

- *visiting the website;*
- *creating an account (with our e-mail addresses, not yours);*
- *adding a link to our website in the profile of the account you just created.*

In some cases there will be a little more work, but nothing too difficult. We have two websites that you will be doing this for so in most cases, you will need to follow the document twice. We require you to provide us with proof that the links have been created for both of our websites by sending us a document with screenshots of our links appearing on the other websites.

This would be an ideal job for a stay-at-home mum or a student looking to make some extra cash. The first month will be a trial period for both you and us and if it all goes well, we'll need someone to do the same thing on a monthly basis thereafter. After we send you the document with the complete instructions, we expect all the links to be completed within three business days (though you could do it in an afternoon). We are offering to pay $50 to complete this job monthly. Please contact us at <youremailaddress> if you're interested.

This way, SEO is handled on the cheap and my sites' search engine results will improve with time, eventually providing even more revenue, while I'm free to pursue other projects.

This leads us to an important rule to live by ...

Your business should pay itself before it pays you

Sure, I could have pocketed the fifty bucks and spent the day diving in Thailand. However, I find solace in knowing this particular stream will only generate more traffic – and revenue – as the links grow. Why eat sprouts when you can grow orchards?

Aside from link building, I also occasionally outsource pay-per-click management (though it can get bloody expensive), small writing projects, and research projects. Keep in mind that I could do all of these myself (I'm a qualified AdWords Advertising Individual who writes 1,500 words a day), but there's only so many hours in a day.

In order to move your business forward, outsource everything but the captain's chair. If you find that you excel at copywriting, then by all means write the sales letters for your products; otherwise, write a draft and pay a professional to complete it for you (or use Instant Sales Letters). The same goes for market research, product creation, split testing, and campaign management.

Build the future from the past

Every stream you build will have components that can be duplicated for future streams. For example, we still use the same landing page and sales page templates featured on our first website, even though they are for very different products. Certain parts of the sales letter, such as the guarantee, call to action, and e-book cover, are boilerplate material that can be used indefinitely. Recommendations for affiliate products can be easily reworded and added to your autoresponder. There's no point to reinventing the wheel with every stream; repeat what works and discard the losers.

Countless authors have used this methodology to create additional works to their existing ones. Once you've created a money-making stream, explain how you did it and sell that information while offering your consultation services for a discount to your readers. Right there, you've created three possible income streams on the back of one stream. Imagine the income potential if you were able to create only a handful of these a year!

Resources for outsourcing:

- **Craigslist** (www.craigslist.org). Post a job and receive offers. Unfortunately, there is no security in place to pay the freelancer.
- **Elance** (www.elance.com). This website allows you to post a job and review bids from freelancers. You can place the funds in an escrow account and release it upon completion. My problem with Elance is with the freelancers: many of them do not complete the job on time, or do a half-assed job. Still, that isn't Elance's fault.
- **Your Man In India** (www.yourmaninindia.com). Great for small projects.
- **Brickworks** (www.brickworks.com). High-end business professionals who can handle a wide variety of services.
- **Ask Sunday** (www.asksunday.com). Pay a set fee for a fixed number of reservation services. If you need a secretary, this is the place to go.

OK, I'VE AUTOMATED MY INCOME AND TRAVELLED THE WORLD ... NOW WHAT?

This is the unexpected snakebite at the end of the journey. After satisfying long-term goals it can be somewhat intimidating when the dreaded question 'Now what?' rears its ugly head. If you're interested in saving more money, you can always get a job that really interests you and allow your streams to fund your retirement account.

There are countless jobs out there designed for people who don't 'do it for the money.'

- **Tour guide** (www.trekamerica.com; www.contiki.co.uk). Arguably the coolest job ever created. You drive through world-class locations with 10 to 20 passengers, basically showing them a great time. You learn, you grow, you party, and you get paid! I worked as a tour guide running tours across the United States, and saw more of the country in three weeks than most people see in a lifetime.
- **National parks.** While this doesn't require travel per se, it is a fantastic way to live in a beautiful place for a season or two. This falls into the 'dirty job, beautiful place' category. For example, you could work as a short order cook in Yosemite (I did) or run the front lobby in Yellowstone. You aren't limited to national parks in the US, just about every country has jobs like these available.
- **Cruises.** If you can stand being on open water for more than a week at a time, working on a cruise ship may be the job for you. Like national parks, cruises require a wide variety of skills, and it's easy to land a job with one.
- **Rafting guide.** Contrary to popular belief, you can be a certified raft guide in a relatively short time (six weeks). Many rafting guides work in one hemisphere for half the year, then move to the other for the remainder. I've known many guides who work in New Zealand and Colorado, and save enough money to travel during their time off.

- **Airline attendant.** Sadly, this is not the glamorous occupation it once was; however, the travel benefits are still there. Flight crew can usually travel for free on their own airline, and get 50 to 75% discounts with other airlines. Generally, rookies work the short-term trips rather than international, so don't expect to go globetrotting at the outset.
- **Dive master** (www.padi.com/english/common/courses/pro/divemaster.asp). If you have a few months, you can take a dive master certification course through a dive shop anywhere in the world. They pay for your room and board, and you are responsible for helping out around the shop while you complete the course. If you love diving, this can save you thousands of dollars on your next trip!

But I don't want to earn minimum wage again!

Before you cry about how little these jobs pay, consider how much money you're *really* earning.

Most of these jobs cover your expenses, allowing you to save the lion's share of your pay. Add on top the amount of income provided by your streams, and you could easily be banking several thousand dollars a month with no expenses. Let's say your business provides roughly $1,500 / £990 per month in passive income, and you land a summer job working in a national park. The park covers your expenses, and you bank around $1,000 / £660 per month. After four months you walk out of the woods with an extra $10,000 / £6,600 in the bank.

If you're with a partner, the numbers are even more exciting. You and your significant other are saving $2,000 / £1,320 per month from working in the park, which, coupled with business income, comes out to $14,000 / £9,240 in the bank at the end of the summer. Suddenly, the pay they offer seems really tempting.

Don't think these jobs are just for college kids either – every age group is represented in these fields (though octogenarians and older may struggle with the scuba diving). Would you rather have a pile of bills and a job at home, or be saving a boatload of cash while living in a place most people pay to visit?

Don't want to work for the man? Freelance

In addition, you will no doubt have harnessed several skills in developing your streams that will prove to be marketable. For example, Darcie freelances as a web designer, I take occasional jobs as an AdWords consultant, and once or twice a year we teach a course on Internet marketing.

How do you market your newfound skills? Darcie and I have had great success with teaching classes. It gives us a chance to demonstrate our expertise in a specific area, while developing potentially long-term relationships with our students. You can also list yourself under the 'Services Offered' section of Craigslist.

There are also a number of websites focused on connecting freelancers with employers. The two most popular are Guru and Elance. Here you can market your services, or outsource parts of your streams to other freelancers.

To learn more about what you can do abroad (or at home) have a look at the following:

- Transitions Abroad magazine: www.transitionsabroad.com
- Meetup: www.meetup.com
- How to become a travel writer: www.writtenroad.com
- Become an English teacher: www.eslcafe.com
- Resources for working abroad: www.workingoverseas.com

ACCESSING MONEY

There seems to be an ongoing debate about the best way to access your funds while travelling abroad. This issue becomes increasingly complex when you are running your own business. Here's what I suggest.

First of all, connect your business account with your personal account. Ideally both of these accounts will be held in the same bank.

Use one credit card to pay for all business expenses. Set it up so the balance on this credit card will be paid automatically each month. My business credit card pays for advertising, autoresponders, web hosting, and product delivery – all while earning some sweet frequent flyer miles.

Use PayPal to accept payments and pay for work that has been outsourced. Make sure to connect your PayPal account to both your personal and business accounts.

Before you leave, purchase as many traveller's cheques as possible via your business account. Contact your bank, which should be able to provide this service for free. Traveller's cheques are accepted around the world and have proven themselves to be the cheapest method for exchanging money.

Once you have your traveller's cheques, write the number of each cheque and e-mail it to yourself just in case you have to report it lost or stolen. A small amount of emergency cash – between $50 / £35 and $100 / £65 – can provide an incalculable amount of peace of mind. Keep your passport and traveller's cheques together – you'll have to show ID to cash the cheques.

You can use an ATM or credit card abroad, but expect service charges both from your provider and the company that is exchanging money for you. The one exception to this is the Capital One card, which waives its fee, but you will still have to pay between 1 and 2% locally.

American Express has recently created a traveller's cheque card, which works like an ATM card and can be refilled at any time.

Cash is always a good option, notwithstanding the obvious risk of losing it.

Money flow

Figure 17 illustrates how the money will flow from your business to fund your travels.

FIGURE 17 **MONEY FLOW**

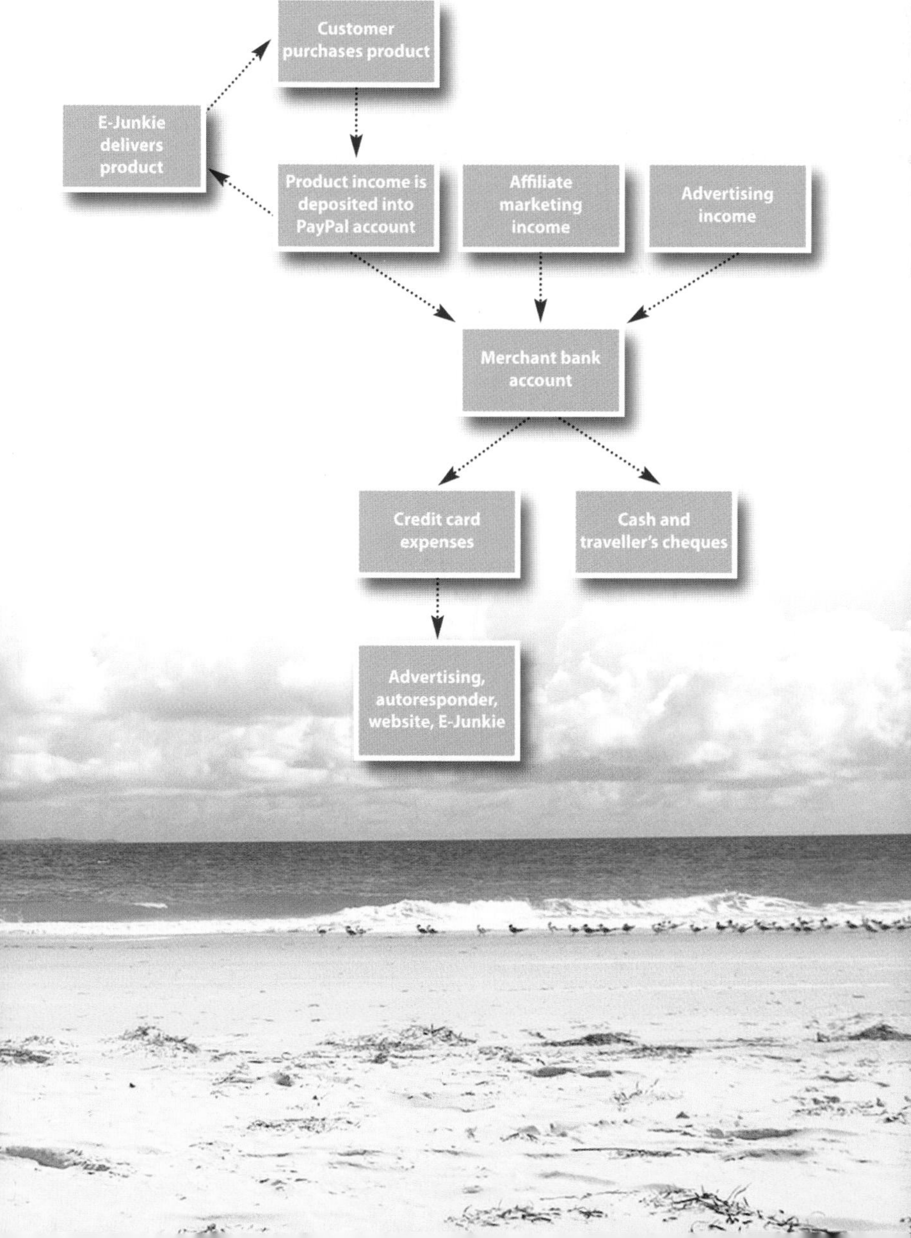

Departure

At this point I feel like a friend saying goodbye at the airport: while unsure of the adventures that lie ahead, I'm excited to see you go. There will be the inevitable ups and downs, the battles against self-doubt, the long hours, and the hard-won lessons that only experience can provide.

Still, when you find yourself at the airport with a plane ticket to adventure in hand, you'll realize it was all worth it.

Darcie and I are living proof that you can escape the rat race and travel the world for as long as you want in less than a year. Looking back, it seemed so hard at the time ... and it was. But now that I know how to create income to fund my lifestyle, those months seemed like the greatest investment I could have made. For you, it will be the same. You have a long hard fight ahead of you, but if you put in the time and create several streams as outlined in this book, you will find yourself at that ticket counter.

You are the author of your dreams ... now it's time to author your reality.

To your success

Adam Costa and Darcie Connell
Ko Lanta, Thailand

PS: I would love nothing more than to hear from you when you book your ticket. Really!

Shift

Glossary

A/B split testing is delivering two different marketing messages in the hopes of improving conversion rates.

AdSense is an advertisement application run by Google. Website owners can enroll in this program to enable text, image, and, more recently, video advertisements on their websites. These advertisements are administered by Google and generate revenue on either a per-click or per-impression basis.

Affiliate advertising is similar to Google AdSense, but in this case an advertiser places an ad on your website and you receive a commission if the prospect goes on to purchase their product.

Affiliate architect stream makes money-building websites that offer prospects numerous different products sold by affiliate partners. A popular example is Amazon, which makes a commission on every product sold.

Affiliate marketing is where a product developer pays commissions on sales to another party for marketing their product.

Article marketing is submitting original pieces of writing to article directories for syndication, where other websites can republish your article with a link to your site.

Autoresponder is a method of automatically e-mailing timed and customized messages at predetermined intervals.

Backlinks are incoming links to a website or web page. In the search engine optimization (SEO) world, the number of backlinks is one indication of the popularity or importance of that website or page (though other measures, such as PageRank, are likely to be more important). Backlinks are also known as incoming links, inbound links, inlinks, and inward links.

Business is an umbrella term which includes numerous streams of passive income.

Click-through-rate (CTR) is a way of measuring the success of an online advertising campaign. A CTR is obtained by dividing the number of users who clicked on an ad or a web page by the number of times the ad was delivered (impressions). For example, if a banner ad was delivered 100 times (impressions delivered) and one person clicked on it (clicks recorded), then the resulting CTR would be 1%.

Confirmed opt-in (COI) is when new subscribers ask to subscribe to the mailing list but, unlike with an unconfirmed opt-in, a confirmation e-mail is sent to verify it was really them. Many believe the person must not be added to the mailing list unless an explicit step is taken, such as clicking a special web link or sending a reply e-mail. This ensures that no person can subscribe someone else out of malice or error. Mail stream administrators and non-spam mailing list operators refer to this as confirmed subscription or closed-loop opt-in.

Content creation stream involves creating large, content-rich websites and earning revenue from advertisers. This stream includes researching a topic and adding new, related material to grow a list of subscribers.

Conversion rate is the ratio of visitors who convert casual content views or website visits into desired actions based on subtle or direct requests from marketers, advertisers, and content creators.

Conversion tracking is a way to track when a visitor clicks to a specific page in your website (e.g. when a visitor clicks 'Buy Now' from your sales page and moves to the order summary page).

Cost-per-action (CPA) – sometimes known as **pay-per-action (PPA)** – is an online advertising pricing model, where the advertiser pays for each specified action (a purchase, a form submission, and so on) linked to the advertisement. Direct response advertisers consider CPA the optimal way to buy online advertising, as an advertiser only pays for the ad when the desired action has occurred. An *action* can be a product being purchased, a form being filled, etc.

Cost-per-click (CPC) is the amount of money an advertiser pays search engines and other Internet publishers for a single click on its advertisement that brings one visitor to its website.

Cost-per-impression (CPI) is a phrase often used in online advertising and marketing related to web traffic. It is used for measuring the worth and cost of a specific e-marketing campaign. This technique is applied with web banners, text links, e-mail spam, and opt-in e-mail advertising, although opt-in e-mail advertising is more commonly charged on a cost-per-action (CPA) basis.

Cost-per-mille (CPM) – also called **cost-per-thousand (CPT)** – (in Latin *mille* means thousand), is a commonly used measurement in marketing. It can be purchased on the basis of what it costs to show the ad to 1,000 viewers (CPM). Rather than an absolute cost, CPM estimates the cost per 1,000 views of the ad. Google AdSense uses this as its benchmark metric.

Domain name is the name a visitor types into their URL address bar.

Fractional factorial experiments is testing a sample of combinations of elements.

Full factorial experiment is testing every combination of elements.

Google AdSense displays Google ads on your website and gets a commission when someone clicks on those ads.

Google Analytics helps you measure where your visitors are coming from, and how they interact with your site.

Keywords are terms people search for in search engines.

Landing page, sometimes known as a lead capture page, is the page that appears when a potential customer clicks on an advertisement or a search-engine result link. The page will usually display content that is a logical extension of the advertisement or link and that is optimized to feature specific keywords or phrases for indexing by search engines.

Market research is the process of systematically collecting, recording, and analyzing data about customers, competitors, and the overall market.

Market trend shows how a market performed in the past, giving you an idea of its likely performance in the future.

Meta tags are web page elements that display information about the web page such as title, keywords, and description.

Multivariable testing is where you can test several aspects at a time and know for certain which factors contributed to success, which contributed to failure, and which were non-performers.

Negative keywords are terms you don't want your ads appearing for.

Niche market is a small specialized market within a larger market.

Online payments are payments a user makes for a product or service online rather than in person or through the mail.

Open jaw ticket is an airplane ticket for flights that arrive in one city and depart from another.

Opt-in e-mail is a term used when someone is given the option to receive 'bulk' e-mail, that is e-mail that is sent to many people at the same time. Typically, this is some sort of mailing list, newsletter, or advertising. Obtaining permission before sending such an e-mail is critical because without it, the e-mail is unsolicited bulk e-mail, better known as spam. See definitions of *confirmed opt-in* and *unconfirmed opt-in*.

Organic listings are the websites displayed in search engines that did not pay for advertisements.

PageRank is a logarithmic scale created to measure the relative importance of a website against all other websites on the Internet.

Pay-per-click (PPC) is an Internet advertising model using search engines, advertising networks, and content sites, such as blogs, in which advertisers pay their host only when their ad is clicked. With search engines, advertisers typically bid on keyword phrases relevant to their target market. Content sites commonly charge a fixed price per click rather than using a bidding stream.

Product development stream is developing a product (a good or service) and selling it online. In general, this entails researching a market, developing a product, creating a website, driving traffic to your website, and selling your product.

Product testing involves creating a website designed to sell a product that hasn't been created yet, driving traffic to that website, and recording how many people complete a 'purchase.'

Public domain can be considered the anti-copyright where you can get and use books, images, or audio for whatever purpose you see fit.

Sales letter is the page designed to sell your product. You can have a fantastic product, but you won't earn anything if your sales letter lacks sizzle.

Search engine index are all the web pages that display in the search engines.

Search engine marketing (SEM) is a form of Internet marketing that seeks to promote websites by increasing their visibility in search engine result pages (SERPs). According to the Search Engine Marketing Professional Organization, SEM methods include: search engine optimization (or SEO), paid placement, contextual advertising, and paid inclusion.

Search engine optimization (SEO) is the process of improving the volume and quality of traffic to a website from search engines via 'natural' ('organic') search results. Typically, the earlier a site appears in the search results list, the more visitors it will receive from the search engine. SEO may target different kinds of search, including image search, local search, and industry-specific vertical search engines.

Sponsored links/PPC are the websites displayed by the search engines which are paying advertisement costs.

Stream is a stream of passive income.

Unconfirmed opt-in is when a new subscriber first gives his/her address to the list software (for instance, on a web page), but no steps are taken to make sure that this address actually belongs to the person. This can cause e-mail from the mailing list to be considered spam because simple typos of the e-mail address can cause the e-mail to be sent to someone else. Malicious subscriptions are also possible, as are subscriptions that are due to spammers forging e-mail addresses that are sent to the e-mail address used to subscribe to the mailing list.

Video marketing is marketing your website, product or service through video.

Web hosting is paying a company to 'host' or store your website on their servers.

Recommended Reading

Ferriss, Timothy (2008) *4-Hour Working Week*. Vermillion.

Jacobson, Howie (2009) *Google AdWords for Dummies*, 2nd edn. Wiley.

Kennedy, Dan S. (2006) *The Ultimate Sales Letter*. Adams Media.

Viney, David (2008) *Get To The Top of Google*, NB Publishing

Caples, John, Hahn, Fred E. (1998) *Tested Advertising Methods*, 5th edn. Prentice Hall

About the Authors

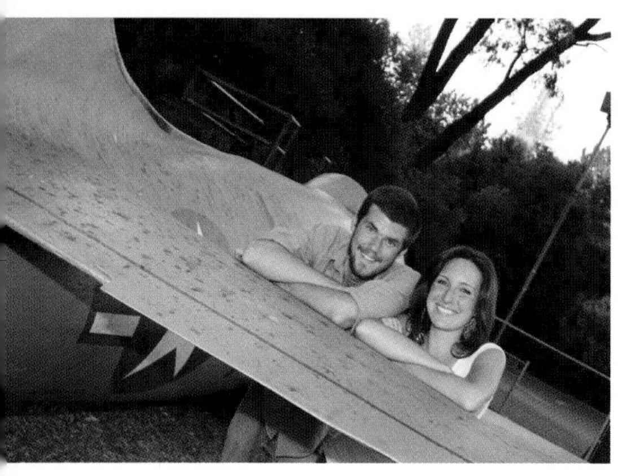

Adam Costa and Darcie Connell have launched over 85 online streams and enjoy most of their time working on the road.

Adam has sung the US and Canadian national anthems at a San Francisco Giants game, participated in a half-time show for the 49ers on Monday Night Football, been deported from Vietnam, lived in Yosemite National Park, worked as a North American tour guide, and studied in New Zealand and Australia. With a degree in Philosophy, he loves nothing more than deep conversation over an even deeper glass of single malt scotch. Before he took his online businesses on the road with him, Adam worked as a travel agent, helping businesspeople plan their international trips.

Darcie has bicycled across Ireland, champagne-tasted in France, hiked through the California redwoods, motorcycled in Vietnam, celebrated at Oktoberfest, bathed in Hungary, tanned in Thailand, and meditated in India, all while making friends along the way. She has a degree in Marketing and extensive work experience in Corporate Training, Business Development, Operations, and Research and Development.

Adam and Darcie teach Internet Marketing courses at more than half a dozen universities around the San Francisco Bay Area. When not living somewhere else, they live in Santa Clara, California. Visit Adam and Darcie on the web at www.stream-life.com.

Index